The Billionaire Right Next Door

You can visit us at:

www.billionairerightnextdoor.com

Dany Tremblay, 1975

Success in business, Billionaire, Wealth

ISNB 978-0-9940074-0-7 (e-book)

ISBN 978-0-9940074-2-1(paper version)

This book is dedicated to Chantal, my special wife, who is always there for me. Behind every successful man you will find a woman. This has been true for me throughout my journey. I also dedicate it to my lovely son Vincent, the sunshine of our family, always happy, smiling and full of energy. Without a doubt, my family is what makes me rich in the first place, and does so every day. They are truly my driving force.

Table of Contents

INTRODUCTION

Have you ever wondered how someone can go from being a virtual nobody to driving down the highway at top speed, taking the exit ramp of success and becoming the next billionaire right next door? Could YOU be sitting behind the wheel of that car? Or is it just a ridiculous fantasy?

Tell me: why do some people actually work on this ambitious plan, while the vast majority think it's just not for them? Is it because they lack ambition, or just because they are unaware of their own potential? These are valid questions...And many similar questions cross my mind when it comes to discussing how wealth is created. I have a passion for great success stories. I crave them. I would even devote my entire life to sharing my knowledge and experiences with the world free of charge.

That way, everybody could make their dreams come true on a grand scale. You will probably immediately answer: it's impossible for everyone to be rich. I would answer right back that you are wrong. Being rich means investing in ourselves and putting our full potential to work on a daily basis. This book is not about get-rich-quick principles and advice. In fact, I am sick and tired of reading the same kind of book over and over, packed with the same old meaningless *blah blah blah*. I personally think many people just use a "cut and paste" technique, lifting from other books, changing a few words and slapping their name on the front page. This message is for all writers who do that: If I can't learn anything new in your book, that's because it isn't your book - it came from someone else. Ahhhh... thank you, it feels good to get that off my chest.

Have no fear, you will not see any "cut and paste" here, and the reason is quite simple: I don't believe that you and I would profit from it. Instead, I will offer you real business opportunities (yes you read that correctly: real ones). Best of all, these are for everyone, no matter how young or old, no matter how much cash you have available. If you prefer to remain a salaried employee (with a weekly paycheck), I also have exclusive opportunities waiting for you in the coming Diamond Heads chapter.

Two years ago, I wrote my first successful book: The 50 Secrets of My Success. At the end, I shared my Wish List of goals I had yet to accomplish. I will give you a complete update on that list, but I can already tell you most of those goals are now part of my daily reality. Did I work harder, 24 hours a day, 7 days a week? Actually, yes and no. As you will see, my recipe for success has not changed much. Of course, I've added some new ingredients to reach a whole new level of success. I will reveal and share the smartest tools I used in the past two years. This way you can duplicate them all and make things happen in your own life. If that's not enough, I will spend an entire day taking you through my routine so that you can watch the whole process in action. Stay tuned for more details later.

Please stay inside this bubble for as long as you can. The goal is to feel as if we were making the trip alongside one another (don't put your book down until you master the process). It is a privilege for me to have you on board. Don't be surprised if you end up feeling in complete control of your life. I will try my best to prod you when necessary, and at times act like your teacher, but please be aware: I am not a motivational guru. I build successful businesses and make them grow over the years. Indeed, deep down inside, I would describe myself as a businessman more than anything else. Sometimes, though, I feel an extreme urge to share special knowledge with others. Believe me, when you enjoy your first taste of success, the very first thing you will want to do is celebrate, live it up. After a life of parties, you will feel like life has given you a tremendous amount. The next step is to give back, and that is exactly what I am doing right now. I hope you will feel that generosity over the coming chapters. I will try hard to give you the very best of me.

Please get ready to buckle up your seat belt, as we are entering a high-speed world: my world, lightning-fast (or speed-on-steroids, if you prefer). I am ambitious by nature, and my goal is to give you the drive you need to move forward to the next level of your life. If we can do this together, I will have succeeded in my mission. Down the road, if you are winning, I am winning as well. Now, you will probably ask yourself the question: can a guy like this really make me a Billionaire? I think that answer is up to you to determine. I am confident I have absolutely everything it takes to make anybody a millionaire.

Becoming a billionaire is just the next step beyond. To answer the question: you can absolutely become whoever you want to be. If a million dollars is all it takes for you to feel great, then rest assured, once you accomplish that, you will want to continue further down that road to success. It's just part of human nature to always want more and explore new avenues. There is very little you can do about this natural and powerful drive that already exists within you. In the coming chapters, I will sometimes refer to my first book, but you don't actually need to read it first. If you feel a critical need to know all the details of my life from the very beginning, then go ahead and start there, but it is not an absolute necessity. Let's begin this journey, but before the fun part, here are the habitual legal notifications. We want you to seek professional advice suited to your personal profile and unique financial situation before deciding to take any action. Keep in mind the publisher and the author are not responsible for any actions or results taken afterwards.

UP WE GO...

I am delighted and excited that you have chosen to join me on this First Class flight. I invite you to climb aboard and find a comfortable seat; the pilot is going through his final checks. We will spend this entire trip together, and I will ask you right off the bat to consider this shared experience as though we were one entity.

The very first thing I do when I want to successfully accomplish major goals is to select some contemporary songs that will send my energy level soaring through the roof. I think you should do exactly the same thing. What is the relationship between success and music? A lot of it has to do with the inspirational power of words and rhythms. Have you ever heard a song and suddenly felt like you were powerful and standing on top of the world? And as a bonus, in total control of your desires to achieve anything? Well, you weren't dreaming: music has the special power to propel us to the stars. On the other hand, when a sad song is playing, a weak feeling can overcome you very quickly. Be careful in how you draw up your Hit List.

When a song is not driving me to achieve great things, I immediately switch to another radio station. On the other hand, if a really good one is working, I crank the volume up to the max. With that level of sound, I feel like I am sending a strong signal to my brain and every cell in my body, telling them: immerse yourself completely and feel deeply enough to remember what this music means to my spirit, drive, dreams and aspirations. Listening to inspiring music while I write is one of the best tools in my arsenal. The goal is to drive my creativity to a maximum level.

Trust me, if I were to listening the daily news report and writing at the same time, the overall result would probably end up being dark and negative. I like to be surrounded by a protective bulb of happiness and positive vibrations. In my opinion, newspapers and TV are a great waste of time, trash and garbage for the soul. Of course, that's just my personal opinion. In the next chapters of the book I will try my best to go straight to the point. I feel very privileged to consider myself a person who thinks for himself. My opinions are not linked to political ideas or influential, controlling figures. My success is entirely self-made. I take great pride in it. The title of this chapter was inspired by and is dedicated to my favourite inspiring song of the moment: Up We Go by Lights (aka Valerie Poxleitner). Please take a few minutes of your time to program the song on your music device and listen to it with your eyes closed.

Don't watch the video of your inspiring song. Official videos of songs stifle your imagination. Stop reading the book until you've listened to the entire song; otherwise, you will lose a great part of the meaning. Now, how do you feel? Don't you agree the song is a powerhouse, that it generates tremendous energy? I think of it as the turbo processor of my craziest, wildest dreams. The beat is almost everything - much more than lyrics. What I like most is when the song is just at the point where the beat is about to explode.

Then, you can hear the repeated phrase, "Everyone here is ready to go..." When I hear it, I feel like I am rising quickly to a point where there is absolutely no limit in my life: the places where all my goals are real and achieved. Of course, that moment is short-lived, but it reminds me of where the destination is and what it looks like. You can link many things to music (good and bad feelings) but I strongly suggest that you to find songs that synch up with your future planned successes. That way, each time you hear the song, it will be like visiting your future, a reminder of how good it feels to be in this magical place. Remember, your mind doesn't know this is fiction - your mind believes it is real. Play the game of music and let the song propel you wherever you want to go in an instant. If you don't mind, I will mention a song in every chapter that perfectly reflects its central idea. It would be a great idea to save them in your billionaire i-pod file. I love to be inspired by music; I think it's is the quickest and best way to drive creativity and energy.

BE YOUR OWN HERO

Without us noticing, our jet has taken off. Time flies when we are together. "Be Your Own Hero" is the title of this chapter, and for a good reason. You must take control of your own life right now before we go any further together. If you are already successful in business, then congratulations, but something tells me your path and mission are not fully completed yet. Somewhere along the road, did you choose to put your car into cruise-control mode? This message applies to almost all of you: please wake up before it's too late. Your life is there, waiting for you. You read that right. Life is waiting patiently for you because you deserve to have an amazing time on Earth. But patience has its limits, as everyone knows.

If you've been living in a gilded cage, with a nice steady job for years now, I have an important message to deliver: life will almost never, ever reward you. Worse, you will feel unfulfilled and increasingly unsatisfied with your lot in life. I can already see your hard-working profile, the kind of person who wants to make a living and protect what's already been accumulated over the years. Meanwhile, you're frittering away the main reason for your time on Earth. I will remind you, but you already know this deep inside: to create. When we create, we feel more alive and happy. Have you ever noticed this eternal fact? It's very difficult to remain in the same job position for years and feel like you are making the most of yourself. Not long ago, I discovered that we are all capable of achieving much more than we think. When we create, we are in perfect symbiosis with our inner self. At the same time, we are in symbiosis with our Bigger Picture, which is to constantly grow and learn. Each time you act this way, life will reward you. If you don't feel you can create anything, what about your children? Weren't you involved in creating them? And if you don't have children, you probably have a closet stuffed with some drawings or writings you did in school many years ago. Who created these drawings? Could the answer be: YOU? Last year, my best friend discovered that he had a creative gift for restoring old, damaged automobiles. He now feels much better every time he is involved in a new bodywork transformation project. This same friend was living in a depressed state the year before he made his discovery, but you'd never know it today.Here's my personal view on the subject. Let's pretend you have a teenager at home who sits on the couch all day long. Will you reward his behaviour by saying: here's a gift son, I am proud of you? No: you'll probably do the opposite.

Now, here is the one hundred dollar question: why should life respond differently towards you when it comes to your gilded cage of a job? Life and your inner self are perfectly aware of your real and full potential. You can do better. Of course your teenager will give you a thousand reasons for sitting around on the couch, just as you will to explain why you stay where you are. You can tell me your thousand reasons over and over, but it will not change the fact that you are wasting the most precious currency you have, which you will never get back: time. On top of that, you are operating at a very low potential rate. If I had to choose between the two, I would far prefer the lazy teenager sitting on the couch for a day than an entire life wasted on a safe, secure job.

I have already told you that I would prod you at times. Honestly, I have no other choice. If you have not set your mind on the idea of going out into an absolutely limitless world, there is very little I can do. To deserve success, you must chase and want it badly enough. On the other hand, if you are ready to travel to the next level of your life, you are in the right place. Our plane is gaining altitude, traction and momentum. Ask yourself this question frequently to verify if you're on the right track: do I feel my life is gaining altitude, traction and momentum? The way we feel is behind everything. You want money because it's great to eat out in a fancy restaurant and travel to Hawaii, and treat yourself like a billionaire. I can easily understand this concept, because simply stated, I think the same way. When my wife and I are on a cruise, we are like kids on Christmas morning, waiting for the sun to set so we can linger on the balcony of our room. We focus on these moments, listening to the sound of waves crashing on the hull of the ship. It's a special time, when we feel like we are on top of the world and the most privileged people on earth. We feel our billion cells vibrating together in perfect harmony with the universe. This is why money is so great; it offers us unique opportunities to experience moments like these.

All the things you want in life are motivated by the good feelings offered by your experiences. Be your own hero now, based on the fact nobody else will. Don't wait to be rich before starting to act and creating your perfect life. Life will reward you based on what you are giving now, not tomorrow or in a place called: Someday. Do you know how I spend my days? I often think, how can I give more to more people? Operational excellence in my business then becomes a possibility. If we provide better service, chances are people will notice it and tell their friends how great they were treated. If we can make fewer mistakes, this also means we offer our guests a better experience. How can we achieve this goal? That is the real question.

Usually, when you ask questions, you can find the answers right around the corner. However, we have to notice them. Do you know why most people fail? They never ask themselves important questions. It's very easy to ignore problems, because all we need to do is stick our heads in the sand, right? It doesn't require much effort. Believe me, this is a very dangerous way of doing business and running your life in general. Your competition will notice your weaknesses and profit from them faster than you can imagine. Let's get back to the point: have you decided to become your own hero and create the life of your dreams? You will create something anyway, good or bad, so why not choose to create great things? If you still believe you are not a creative force, then put down this book and completely clear your head. There is really nothing we can do until you have decided to act in this manner. No, I will not refund the price of this book if you have decided to stay where you are in life for the sake of your family. There are plenty of reasons to not succeed out there. Frustration will be your reward every time. You've probably heard this a thousand times: there is always a solution to each problem. So why are you still carrying your ugly list of reasons to keep from becoming the person you really want to be? Wanting to become billionaire is great, but if this is not enough for you, simply ask more. Welcome aboard to all those brave readers who want to continue this magical journey and achieve their greatest and wildest dreams.

We are not returning to the departure lounge. Those who've changed their minds and want to go back will find a couple of parachutes on board. Strap one on if this adventure is not for you. We will open the doors and you can exit right now, but I would ask anyone to reconsider before deciding to leave. The perfect song for this chapter is: Follow Me by Uncle Kracker. Follow me and you will never regret your decision.

IT'S TIME FOR PIZZA...

The typical American loves pizza, and I can easily understand why. Let's face it, pizza is the perfect meal because you can easily share slices with friends and loved ones. Add in the other advantages – it's quick, inexpensive, delicious and doesn't require forks, knives or even plates! – and what could be better? That's probably why pizza is so synonymous with success. When it's time to build up your new business ideas, always think of the Pizza Process. The good news is that you don't necessarily need to sell pizza or even like it at all to make profitable use of this tool. The concept is quite simple: all great new business projects come front-loaded with tons of different steps required to transform the dream into a reality. This is way too much for your brain to handle all at once. Most of the time, your brain will quickly kill off your dream by reminding you of the complications involved and the almost impossible level of work.

Your brain is right. But what if we take out our pizza slicer and cut the project into six separate slices? That way, we have the unique opportunity to re-approach the brain with a brand new deal. The deal is to look at each slice as representing one of six separate projects (don't tell your brain you will reassemble the pieces into a single whole again at the end). Here is your ideal sales pitch: listen brain, I've got this little project. It's only a small slice, no big deal. I can easily do this without burning myself out. Your brain will probably agree right away. Next, for the best shot at success, choose the easiest slice at first. This is not a joke: this tool really works. And don't assume it's all too simple to be true. Simple things usually work, precisely because of their extraordinary simplicity.

I'd hazard the guess that at least once in your life, you had a million- or even billion-dollar idea. Everybody does. Please return to that special moment in your life, remember it, and tell me: what happened to your great idea? In the beginning, you were convinced it was a great moneymaking project – so why did you kill it off? My guess is that the idea was too big, unwieldy and complicated for your already busy everyday life. What you need to realize is that successful, wealthy people have become so by executing the proper follow-through on their ideas. You don't have to believe me right off the bat. Just invest a few hours in studying the lives of people who have accomplished things, and draw your own conclusions. You will witness this process in action. They all attacked the first step, solving roadblocks and problems, then moved forward to the next pizza slice. In my view, this is the only way to stay focused and pursue projects or great ideas to their successful completion. I learned the Pizza Slice Principle back in 2010. It was a critical time period, when everyone involved in one of my restaurants was overwhelmed, running around like headless chickens to no great effect.

My manager offered me an idea: Why don't we try the Pizza Process and give one slice apiece to each of the best-trained and most talented team members. One slice would be focused on morning drive-through target monitoring. Another would address precise weekly inventory. The goal was to be better positioned to control our food costs by perceiving opportunities more clearly. The next slice would involve training new team members and upgrading and maintaining the existing ones. The last slice would center on performing daily checkpoint controls of the chain's standards. I was skeptical at first, but told my manager to move ahead and test the concept. One month later, the results were remarkable: the restaurant was back on its feet in record time, with strong growth momentum. The level of engagement of our team members had skyrocketed to previously unseen heights. All credit goes to my manager Ian Bastien for his great stroke of initiative. And believe me, in the future I will always remember to apply this successful method for achieving great results. The perfect song for this chapter is: One In A Million, by David Myles. Be that one in a million, use this simple technique, and you will generate great results.

APOLOGY

Sometimes in life, we make mistakes. Afterwards, we feel like we have to own up to it and resolve the issue by apologizing. That is exactly what I plan to do in this chapter. But have no fear, there will be a great bonus gift in it for you. I had never in my life read a book that offered me real business opportunities. This book was written to be different. I will share many other real opportunities with you, so please stay tuned until the end. My goal is to have a real impact in your life. I may be repeating myself here, but this book is not about success principles, but more about doing real pay off deal. Becoming a billionaire involves accumulating business successes and capitalizing on them over time.

My own list of apologies begins with my first book, The 50 Secrets of My Success. I opened one early part of the book by mentioning legal contracts that were still in effect with my franchisor. Due to that situation, I thought I would not be allowed to mention the name of my business brand franchise. Then, when the book was released, I quickly realized my fears of blowback from the head office were greatly exaggerated and existed only in my mind. As you already know, the first inkling of fear we experience is usually quite small. Next thing you know, that little fear has been transformed into a mountain. In many such instances, the fear only exists in our minds, not in the real world.

I drew one central conclusion from that experience: we rarely get blowback when we say complimentary things about the person or company involved. Having left their name out in a misperception of the situation, I was left with regret, because success started to work its way into our lives the day my wife and I signed the franchise contracts. In other words, it was almost like neglecting to give any credit to your parents for having become the person you are today. Our parents have a great influence in our lives, no doubt about it, and the same has been true of my relationship with Tim Hortons. I made the best and wisest business decision I ever have on the day I joined this great brand. I hereby offer my gratitude to the universe for this amazing gift. Over the years, Tims has given me an incredible opportunity to develop the business skills required, with all the necessary support from the corporate team at the head office. In 2001, I had the drive and willingness to be a businessman, but none of the experience. It's like the first day you try to ride a bicycle. We can learn anything, but it's scary at first, isn't it?

Wherever you live in the world today, especially in the U.S., you can witness the booming expansion of the Tim Hortons brand... and a franchise will probably landing in your community sooner than you think. I am not here to sell you anything, much less so to offer you any legal advice. It's your job to seek advice and formulate your own opinion. But let's just say opportunity is knocking for those who would love to become the next franchisee and own a piece of this great worldwide quick-service leader. This merits your closer consideration. I mean, look at how well it all turned out for me – why couldn't that happen for you? Success is generated by the Tims formula when owners work hard, are involved in their community and follow the rules of the system. Moreover, if you have your eye on expansion (if you are doing a great job) your next step could be a multiple-franchise business model.

The procedure is simple: you pick up the phone, as I did, and ask for the application forms to be mailed to your home address. Nowadays, of course, you can do this online. If you receive a follow-up call for an interview, you must be ready to make your finest pitch, selling yourself as the next best franchise owner in the

Tims chain. Don't forget that if the company signs you on, you will have to demonstrate all those claims from the interview. Of course, as when buying a house, you need a cash down payment to qualify, and you need a bank loan. Gather information on the minimum requirements. If you don't yet have all the cash for the down payment available, your next critical task is finding the money.

Almost nobody has all the money at first, as was the case with me. I worked like crazy to find ways to resolve this missing money problem. To make our dream a reality, my wife and I had no choice but to return to living in a small apartment for the first two years. You can find all the details of that story in my first book. It's very important to have mentors or inspirational people to help drive you forward. When I entered the chain back in 2001, I was lucky enough to encounter just such a driving force almost instantly. His name is David Clanachan, a guy with so much energy and passion he can practically move mountains by himself.

Imagine this scenario: he entered the company as a night shift baker. By 2001, he was already managing the training center and training store in Oakville where I was undergoing my own training. I remember that he was always moving at top speed, with the utmost level of confidence. He could convince a listener of anything right away because he knew the art of choosing powerful words matched with the uniquely passionate tone of his voice. He didn't know at the time (he does now) but I identified him as my perfect inspirational model in my own process of integrating myself into the business. In the year after my training period, David was promoted to vice-president in the company hierarchy. I was very happy for him (and for me, too). I knew he deserved his promotion and was the right man in exactly the right position. Every year, he inspired all of us franchisees to drive ourselves further down the road to success, alongside his own mentor our legendary president and CEO, Paul House. If you would like to consider becoming part of the Tim Hortons family, I would first advise you to experience the chain as a guest. You have to fall in love with the products and the brand concept. The next step is to speak with different owners directly, armed with a pointed and clear list of your own questions. Remember, any success you can achieve in this business genre is directly linked to your social skills and the way you connect with your guests and team members. I hope we can one day welcome you as part of the franchisee family. Thousands of guests have approached me over the years to say they can't quite put their finger on it, but there is something special and unique at Tims. My answer has never changed: it is because the owners of Tim Hortons franchises fill their restaurants with a driving, passionate energy that radiates beyond the location into the community itself. Leadership and innovation are part of the company DNA, and we take pride in that. It is an enormous privilege to be part of a great venture that is bigger than us. Last summer, the worldwide convention was held in Toronto, assembling 5000 supremely galvanized folks, thrilled not just about what we had achieved over the past 50 years, but also for the bright future ahead of us. We are unique because deep down in our hearts, we know exactly who we are, which is why our clientele love us so much. If I had to sum up the Tims model in just a few words, I would say: pride, and giving back to our communities.

And then I would add a few more crucial adjectives: bold, daring and different. I would like to end this chapter by sharing a song that represents how much I love the Tim Hortons brand: the beautiful song called A Thousand Years, by Christina Perri.

I LOVE DETROIT

At this early point in our journey, with the example of the previous chapter, I hope you can see how devoted I am to helping you down your future road to success. Now let's push further, into real estate. You already know who Donald Trump is and how much money he's made over the years in real estate. That is my story too, especially since 2009, the year I started to build my U.S. real estate portfolio. In just a short period of time, I was able to invest in 6 different U.S. states.

One of my favorites is Michigan, for one obvious reason: attractive rent-versus-price ratio. Everyone around me said I was crazy to invest there, so one day, I stopped wasting time talking about it, and started to buy. When it comes to investing my money, one of my favorite strategies is to head in the exact opposite direction of the masses. Believe it or not, that's always resulted in my most profitable deals. Prices are at rock bottom and as an added bonus, competition is almost nonexistent. I love Detroit, even though I've never even been there. The city has a very special history. Detroit was very successful and prosperous until the year 1967. Then, a series of racial, social and labor crises exploded everywhere like a virus. These events were enough to propel the city through a series of municipal misfortunes. Next, just to make matter worse, some of the city's mayors were found guilty of illegal misuse of funds.

The city was plunged into what seemed to be an endless downward crash. Manufacturers were closing down one after another like a house of cards. There seemed to be no light at the end of the tunnel. People started to leave the city for a better one.

The final devastating event came in 2008 during the financial crisis, when the Big Three automakers asked President Obama for a bailout. At that point, real estate prices on virtually every building took a major nosedive into what seemed to be a bottomless pit. No doubt about it, the situation was extremely critical. When the city protected itself against its creditors and filed for Chapter 11 in 2010, I was not surprised. How can you uphold your financial obligations when there is so little money coming in on the treasury side? But that's the beauty of America. When someone fails THAT big, it's possible to erase the entire mess and start over. I think this was the best, wisest decision, and to me, it seemed like the beginning of a new era. That was when I began investing my money and receiving an amazing return. There is still a fortune to be made in Detroit in the coming years and decades. If you're thinking about looking into this market and want to be successful, here is some of the advice I can share.

First, you must visualize the Detroit area as being like a donut. The hole in the center is the downtown and financial district. Since the famous federal bailout of GM, Ford and Chrysler, things have gotten back to normal on the business side. There are good jobs to be found again as well. In a way, the downtown district is on a nice recovery mode curve. Some businesses from outside Michigan have also seen a solid opportunity and moved their U.S. head offices there at a bargain price.

But the rest of the donut (outside the city center) is still a bad area – the one you can only see in Hollywood movies. Until you get beyond the famous 8 Mile Road, I would say it is way too early to even think of doing anything. Some companies will try to sell you a house for 15K. This is a bad investment move because you will never find a quality tenant in an area like that. Furthermore, insurance premiums will also be a problem. If you can find one company willing to insure a house there, your premiums will devour a big chunk of your rent – assuming you've been lucky enough to find a tenant to pay it. And as you can well imagine, crime rates are still through the roof. If you look beyond 8 Mile in suburban towns like Livonia, Dearborn and Eastpointe, you will find great investment deals and quality tenants. People who work goods job at auto manufacturing plants don't live in Detroit. Wise investors know, and go where families with good jobs are.

One great company I would recommend for outside investors is Michigan Property Management. You enlist them to help you buy investment properties. Once done, they will help you to get your house ready to rent, and find a qualified tenant (with screens and criminal background checks). The company then collects rental revenue for you, keeping a 10% management fee. Finally, if you want to sell part of your portfolio someday, they can also handle that. All the services can be found under one roof, which is what I like and what I am looking for as an outside investor. Depending on the time of year, I live in West Palm Beach or Honolulu. Without a management company like that, it would be impossible for me to invest long-distance in properties far from my home. Readers often want to know: if jobs have returned to Michigan, why haven't real estate prices recovered back to pre-crisis levels? First of all, prices are back on the upswing. Since late 2012, prices in general have stopped falling and the curve has begun swinging in the other direction.

Second, real estate has a lot to do with human confidence in the future. It's fairly easy for an outsider like me to say things are improving and tons of money will be made from now on. If you speak to a person who lived through the recent crisis there, you will then understand. The trials and tribulations of the crisis are still fresh in their minds. I am not sure you would have the same level of optimism or positive view of the future if you had been stuck in the midst of that storm. You see, we all tend to project our future lives based on what we have experienced in recent years.

Real estate is not yet an attractive and sexy subject for them. Remember that people there watched the value of their homes slashed in half in record time. The last reason is that many people lost their bank credit at the same time they were losing their homes during the crisis. Recovering your credit takes time – between 5 to 7 years, depending on each individual case. During all this time, thousands of people who lost their bank credit haven't been able to buy property, even if they have found a good job. On the other hand, they are looking for a house to rent. If you take on the strategy of buying and holding for at least 5 years, you will make very good returns on your investments. I can see better days ahead for Michigan in general, no doubt about it.

I like the fact that people have stayed there despite a brutal economic situation. Those are resilient people, and if you ever visit the city, don't be surprised to see Detroiters on the street wearing t-shirts with a raised middle finger. They wear it with pride, because I think they consider it a gesture of defiance and vengeance against the rest of the world. It's a way for them to say: we were beaten down and humiliated many times over the past few decades (and honestly, they have seen it all) but we are strong. This battle is far from over. We will never ever give up until we have succeeded once again.

I like that hero-warrior attitude. I admire them, which is why I like Detroit so much. The city is an extraordinary example of resilience, despite everything that has happened in the past. Yes, you would be correct in reminding me that almost all of the buildings are still run-down. However, I don't like to look at things as they are right now; rather, I see how amazing they can become, and the opportunities that lay ahead. I'm pretty good in predicting future events. I'm betting that if they continue the way they're going, seeing the future as filled with opportunity and promise, they will start hitting home runs again. I only have this to say to the countries of the world that laughed at Detroit, said it was finished and that it would be better to close it all down: *never* underestimate the American people. When everyone is pessimistic, calling you crazy for ideas and investment decisions, don't worry too much about it: stick to your plan. Those are always the moments when most money is made. Does that make you think I'm some kind of investment shark? I must admit I like it when there's a lot of financial "blood" in the water, but honestly, I see it differently. When you are investing in a depressed market, you are actually helping to improve it, one drop at the time. It's all about offer and demand, and the more demand, the better the market recovery. That's why we are so hugely rewarded. If you are interested in getting serious about investing in real estate, there are many viable locations across the U.S. Chances are, you will make good money almost everywhere. Just remember that you must choose cities where jobs are available. You can read my first book if you would like to learn more about how to crunch the numbers and analyze a city. In this book I will only urge you to buy your first investment property. The first deal is always the hardest to close. Fear of making mistakes will be there, haunting your thinking. However, the next investment will be a familiar repeat process.

You may want a mentor or a coach to guide you at first. Not a bad idea. But if you don't the have money required to invest, don't waste time beating yourself up. Everyone has to start somewhere. Instead, find folks who don't have the time and know-how to invest, but have the money available. Then, sell your expertise and start signing joint venture partnerships. Basically, a joint venture partnership involves one partner who has time and expertise available, and another partner who has money but no available time. Usually, this partner wants a better return on his investment than the 0.5% interest he normally earns on his bank account. Your partnership agreement contract should contain all the details: the role each will play and the terms both of you have decided upon. The profit is usually divided in half. Let's say you purchased a house at 100K with a partnership agreement and were able to resell it at 200K four years later. You would have just made a killing with literally $0 investment from your own pocket. Now let's pretend you are very good at this, and have 20 joint ventures up and running with different partners. Do you think you could become a millionaire spending $0 from your pocket? You'd better believe it... but of course, the process would require plenty of work and time on your part. You will never make anything unless you first have something to offer from your side: that's the way life works.

To this date, some 25 readers have told me about their own successful joint ventures. They did all of it on their own because they were on fire and hungry to eventually become millionaires. I had not done the work for them, and they took great pride in telling me their success stories. Here is the $64,000 question: what about you? At the very least, please think about it. Something tells me you picked up this book because you want to succeed. Success is like a pretty yet shy woman: you have to work very hard to get her attention. The next step after that is to win her heart. If you want to make real estate deals and would like a second opinion, our team of coaches will be happy to assist you. I have not written much here about flipping houses. I know it's a subject many people are interested in learning more about. However, as with the stock market, I am not a strong believer in shortcut profits. I know that strategy can generate success, but I also know it takes an incredible amount of effort, simply because the timeframe is too short. Of course, TV shows on real estate flipping are very funny and cool to watch.

Have you noticed that some horrible and unsuspected tragedy always occurs in each episode? And yet at the end, out of nowhere, the story has 99.9% happy ending. I will tell you this: I highly doubt the financial numbers they offer us at the end are real. If I'm wrong, good for them, but from my viewpoint, this is nothing more than a TV "reality" show – using the word "reality" loosely. Don't kid yourself, real life is vastly different from TV – especially if your flipping strategy doesn't sell as you had originally planned. Believe me, the bills will be coming in fast and furious.

Your plan to turn a 50K profit can suddenly go up in smoke. Personally, I'm not a fan of gambling, because there's no guarantee that I will win, and I consider house-flipping to be a kind of casino bet. However, as you will read in the next chapter, flipping houses on TV can make for great viewing indeed.

FLIPPING IN THE USA

If you've got a minute, I'd like to share a special story with you. This is one of the more relaxing and fun chapters in the book... unless you are a TV producer. I hope you enjoy it – life must be fun, because too much seriousness is bad for your heart.

This true story concerns my brother Gino and me. Last year, we created a new reality TV project together. The script concept involved an annual TV contest in flipping houses across America, with a grand prize of one million dollars going to the big winner. The TV concept was originally created for a major network, such as Fox or ABC. The idea was to make each week a competition between two specially selected experienced participants. A regular season would run 10 to 12 weekly episodes every year. Now imagine a script that opens like this: my brother and I are each driving around in our Ferraris (after all, we are successful businessmen in real life). My brother's roadster is black, mine is red. The two brothers at the head of this show are naturally competitive. As the show begins, we are driving alongside one another to the West Palm Beach airport to pick up our two new contestants. We then bring them to an initial briefing at our respective homes.

Once at the house, the participants are presented to the TV audience and briefly explain their previous experience in flipping houses – both good and bad. Next, each coach gives his contestant a house project to flip, with a location city, budget and time limit. With one contestant assigned to my team and the other to my brother's, our role is to guide them through the entire flipping process. The contestant winner in each episode is the one who successfully flips the house within the time limit, with the maximum profit margin relative to the initial price of the house. After the initial briefing, we bring them both back to the airport, where they catch a flight to the city where the flip project has been planned. A cameraman films the participants at all times. The cameraman is responsible for capturing the evolution of each project and reporting back to us regularly, so that we can guide each participant and follow their progress from home. Needless to say, my brother and I would not be wasting our own time while our contestants are away working on their projects. We would be working on our own real business deals elsewhere, with every deal featured as part of the reality show. Every deal would be different, evolving around our different partners in each episode.

When time runs out, our contestants have to stop everything immediately. The goal is to see if the two properties have been sold, and how much profit has been made. Our two contestants then return to our house in West Palm Beach for a briefing on the final results, with each coach conducting a thorough review of his contestant's work. Our contestants' mistakes would be part of the review process, along with tips offered for their own future flip projects. Obviously, if one contestant loses money on his project, the coach would be very angry. Hey – it's all part of the show. Profits or losses are officially announced to the audience and the winner pops open a bottle of champagne. The winning contestant is invited to return for another challenging project and a shot at the yearly prize of one million dollars. The season's big winner gets to celebrate in Vegas on top of the Wynn hotel complex, where – drum roll! – the grand prize check is presented.

How do you like the script so far? My brother and I simply loved it, copywriting it and sending it off to a serious TV producer. The producer loved it too. He called us back the next day for a Skype interview, which went well, although the producer informed us that the timing was not good for them and their current schedule. And so our adventure concluded… for now. Things didn't entirely work out for us, but who knows what the future may hold? Another producer may read this book and call us back. It was wonderful to imagine what the show would be like. We were like crazy, excited kids. This chapter was written as an example of how people can dream big in life. Needless to say, dreams don't work out every time, but if you hit a home run on only 3 out of 10 swings, you will undoubtedly be on the road to success.

Have you ever had a script idea like ours? If so, why not write down all the details and copyright your work? It will cost you a grand total of $20 and 15 minutes of your time. Then send a copy to the appropriate producers who have the power to create that kind of show. Hey, you never know. People have sold scripts for huge sums of money. You could be next. We certainly haven't given up on our script idea. Don't be surprised if you turn on your TV one day and see: Flipping in the USA, Season 1 – Coming this spring! Our perfect song for this chapter is: Try, by Colbie Caillat. Whenever you try, you give yourself the power to feel pride in yourself, saying: I gave it my best shot.

DIAMOND HEADS INTERNATIONAL

I hope you have already discovered new ideas to help you become the next billionaire or millionaire – whichever one you choose. We are now flying at full speed 20,000 feet above the ground. Our designated waiter just served us the finest champagne available in crystal glasses. Flying in VIP class has its privileges. We are very fortunate, aren't we? If you are hungry, there's fresh salmon on the menu, or perhaps you'd like to order the juicy 3-inch burger! Please don't eat too much – try to leave room for dessert, because in this chapter you can explore two different kinds of opportunities.

OK, let's get back to serious business. I know that's what interests you. Diamond Heads is the wildest, craziest project I have encountered in my life thus far, and I'm very excited to share all the details with you. Honestly, I feel like a kid in the biggest candy store on Earth. The important question is: are you ready for this? OK, let's go for it, but at the same time I don't want to burn steps. If you are about to turn in for the night, please read this chapter tomorrow. I want you to be at your absolute best before we move on. Believe it or not, everything started very slowly. I was giving a lecture for the release of my first book, The 50 Secrets of My Success, when I suddenly received a message from a reader, telling me how much he had enjoyed his reading experience. He then asked if we could meet at my earliest convenience. I replied we could do so the following week. That week came quickly and we met for lunch as planned. There was a natural connection between us, as Guillaume and his family have been successful in the jewelry business for 27 years. Guillaume Lussier is probably the best jewelry designer in North America today. If you want a gold ring with a one-carat emerald created from your own custom design, he will craft it for you. There is absolutely nothing he cannot accomplish in this domain. He is a high-profile professional man with a special gift, who shows great leadership in everything he does. At lunch, we spent hours talking back and forth nonstop. Then, out of nowhere, he suddenly uttered a pivotal phrase: One day, I will design, produce and sell the most expensive pen on earth. I immediately responded that the day was probably closer than he thought. We both laughed, but I was thinking all the while: could this become a reality?

As lunch ended, Guillaume told me that he and his father were in possession of a large quantity of diamonds, with a pleasant dilemma: they didn't know what to do with them. The cache had been purchased many years previously at bulk price. Best of all, they were already cut; a rough uncut diamond doesn't have the same value. I kept all this in mind and told myself: one day, we will find a way to make use of those diamonds. Before leaving, I questioned Guillaume about the global luxury pen market. He didn't have all the answers, but told me that the world's leading luxury pen company was racking up close to $700 million in sales every year. I was amazed. Nothing else happened for several months, but I never completely forgot our conversation. Slowly but surely, the idea of starting a jewelry business with Guillaume and his family began to cycle through my mind. I started an inner dialogue with these "project spirits," saying: all right, I'll consider this, but we've got to have a strong brand name. I knew it was foolish to even think about succeeding without one. The first step was to write down possible names on a blank sheet. I have to admit that the initial exercise produced nothing of value: the entire list of names I came up with was junk, an absolute guarantee of failure. Eventually, I grew tired of it all. I'd had enough, and set it aside. Nevertheless, the project remained in the back of my mind, constantly nagging at me. I told myself there had to be something to it, had to be something big in this, just waiting for me. The following day is one I will never forget. After waking, I decided for some unknown reason to find some paper clips to tidy up my desk. At that very moment, my eyes were drawn like a magnet to a backup CD from my Sony camera, titled: Diamond Head. The backup CD was a record of our last visit to the Diamond Head volcano in Honolulu, Hawaii. My wife and I had traveled there a few years back and had instantly fallen in love with the place. We'd recorded the entire trip on our camera for posterity. I had burnt the backup CD the day after returning from Hawaii, entitling it "Diamond Head" and storing the copy in my home office drawer. The answer I had been looking for had been sitting there in the drawer for years, just waiting to be re-discovered. Of course, I softly wondered why the name hadn't occurred to me in the first place. In a split second, all those lovely memories of the natural beauty of the volcano were fresh in my mind, as though the trip had happened the day before. My "project spirits" returned as well, whispering: wouldn't it be nice to recreate and capture all that incredible beauty in high-end quality products? The answer was obvious: *YES*. I knew I was on the right track. In all honesty, I had the most extraordinary sensation of butterflies in the stomach.

At dinner that night, I bought a very good bottle of wine. I intended to reveal that morning's vision and the entire project to my wife. I wanted a first outside opinion. My wife Chantal was the perfect person to offer one, because she never hesitates to let me know if one of my business ideas is a non-starter; on the other hand, when a project is promising (let's say, once out of every ten), she responds just as quickly. I was ready to sell the crazy project to her. I started off very vague: Honey, do you remember our trip to Diamond Head volcano? Of course, she responded. Do you remember how beautiful that volcano was? Yes, she answered – do you want to go to Hawaii? I did, of course, but that wasn't the point of the chat. She turned the full focus of her big, beautiful green eyes on me, as though this were the third degree. I had her full attention. You see, my wife knows me very well, and I knew she was thinking: what kind of new idea is he about to reveal me?

Strategically, when I want to sell my wife on a project, I try to make it seem as small and easy as possible. Then, as time unfurls, I slowly but surely reveal each layer, like an onion. Sometimes, this plan works better than others, because my wife is perfectly aware of my savviest tricks. This time, with the Diamond Heads business model, things were different. First, she told me the name was a great one for high-quality products. Second, she was ready to partner with me within five minutes. Believe me, this was not normal, at least not coming from my wife. The process was almost too easy, without the slightest argument. I was amazed!

I mean, I had entered prepared for battle, but found there was no enemy army facing me. My energy level for the project shot through the roof. Initially, the idea had simply been to produce a line of high-end pens, each with a genuine quality diamond. Suddenly, in the back of my mind, I could sense a much larger plan already building for product lines extending to sunglasses, perfume, gold rings, watches, brandy... the expansion was virtually limitless. The next step was to gauge other people's reactions, and the best person for a second opinion was Guillaume, my natural partner for this kind of project. I took the simplest route, calling him and inviting him for lunch. The rendezvous was booked for the following week.

At lunch, I offered almost the same sales pitch as I had to my wife. His reaction was pretty much the same as well. He was easily convinced, liked the name and the concept. He told me he would produce 3 different pen models with a genuine diamond mounted on each. I was in heaven. Time passed. I was busy with my businesses and Guillaume was busy with his jewelry store. Months were slipping by without my pens being delivered. Despite many follow-up calls, nothing happened. I had a lecture to deliver for 60 new and inspiring business people in two weeks. I had planned to talk about the Diamond Heads project and asked Guillaume to send me a prototype at the very least. He confirmed that one would be delivered in time for the lecture. When the prototype arrived, it was not exactly what I had been expecting – which is often the case. Somewhat ruefully, I told Guillaume that we could put the first Diamond Heads pen in the official company museum and share a laugh over it ten years from now.

The lecture went well. The crowd at my presentation was just on fire. They particularly freaked out over the Diamond Heads project, likely because I had taken the time to lay out a detailed business plan for the ensuing ten years. I'm assuming you're curious, so I'll offer the same detailed plan to you right here. The business plan project:

The project has four different business plan phases.

Phase One: Our goal is to sell 1000 high-end pens in our first year. The great advantage in partnering with Guillaume is that Diamond Heads starts off with 120 points of sale in the U.S. and Canada, as we can count on the current sales agent network already in place. Without even having our merchandise on-hand, we were racking up impressive pre-order sales on the pens merely by describing them – at that point, there weren't even any photos available! In Phase One, we will establish our world headquarters in Honolulu, Hawaii. We are currently in the process of leasing a location that meets our requirements. It just makes perfect sense for us to be located near the volcano. We also want to ensure that our products are made in Hawaii for the U.S. market. We believe Americans will reward us for fabricating our products at home, proudly bearing the stamp *Made in Hawaii.*

Phase Two covers Years 2 to 3, when Diamond Heads grows the available product lines: watches, fine brandy bottles, perfumes, custom gold rings, sunglasses and beyond. In this phase, Diamond Heads products will be available for sale in over 50 countries. In

Phase Three, we will introduce our super-luxury product lines, a division called Diamond Headz. The letter Z on the title differentiates this special line. The ultra-luxe line will only produce 20 unique items per year per product. People will have to reserve their products in advance, and there will obviously be a waiting period involved as we produce each work of art. Each Diamond Headz watch will cost approximately $700,000 dollars U.S. In addition, Guillaume will also be busy designing the most expensive pen in the world. However, we will only offer 20 items per year in the exclusive lines. All of these products will be custom-made. If Angelina Jolie wants a 5-carat diamond on her pen... her wish is our command. Moreover, we will physically deliver the product to your door.

Phase Four has a 5-year time frame. We will launch an IPO, introducing the company to the New York Stock Exchange. We will hold 51% of the shares, with the rest made available for public sale. In this phase, Diamond Heads will have a presence all over the world. The company will be making $2 billion in annual sales.

How do you like the business model so far? Do you still believe it's impossible to become a billionaire with a project like this? We have probably now reached the point where your inner question is: what's in it for me? Well, frankly, if you are interested in an executive position, we have the perfect one for you: International Vice President. Diamond Heads is looking to hire the best person for the role, to explore new market and business opportunities. Like any other business, Diamond Heads needs to grow. If you have a strong track record, a wealth of contacts, and experience in the luxury goods industry, we want to hear from you. The starting base salary is $500,000, plus bonuses and benefits. The VP position also requires global travel. Ambition and natural sales talent are must-have attributes. Diamond Heads will need to fill Vice President positions all over the world as the business grows, so even if you read this book two years after its release, we will likely still need more Vice Presidents as we expand – who knows, perhaps in Asia. If you are interested in the position, please send us your resume via the official website www.diamondheads.co We will also need to hire a Chief Financial Officer. If you prefer number-crunching to sales, Diamond Heads CFO may be the role for you. Perhaps if you live in Ohio and are sick and tired of the long winters – just imaging joining us in Hawaii.

We will also have a distribution position to fill at our HQ. If you are a jewelry artist like Guillaume, you may want to think of pursuing your career and craft at Diamond Heads as well. It would be Guillaume's pleasure to host you for an interview in Honolulu. Best of all, if the interview were successful, you could celebrate coming on board in an utterly unique way – by hitting the beach and going surfing. I must tell you right off the bat that our standards are very high – and you would probably have to move to this beautiful paradise… but my guess is that wouldn't be a hardship.

I hope you now feel this book holds real opportunity for you. But please remain seated – remember, we are on a jet together, flying at high speed to the gleaming city of Success. In fact, this is just the first in a long list of opportunities; ultimately, you can choose the one you like most. This next opportunity is for entrepreneurs who are not afraid to go out and get what they want. These are the kinds of people who prefer business income to paychecks. They want more from life… namely, tons of money. This kind of person wants to drive a Lamborghini instead of a Toyota. This groupe loves to fly to Switzerland on a moment's notice for a ski trip, *schuss* down the Alps and sip a cup of hot chocolate next to a roaring fireplace in a million-dollar cottage... Now *this* is living. You likely get the picture. Let's move on – say you live in Dubai. Being a very intelligent businessman, you may want to buy the rights to sell and distribute all Diamond Heads product lines in your country. In business terms, this is known as buying the master franchise for a designated territory. You then turn around and sell all products lines on a massive scale in Dubai. Just imagine – the profit margins are terrific and the possibilities are endless. All I will ask is that you call me before you fly off on your Switzerland trip. That way, if I'm not busy, we can travel together. In all seriousness, this is a huge opportunity, no matter where you live. If you believe in our brand and understand where we want to go, you should consider the offer. If all you want is the Florida territory, give me a call. I will wait patiently for you, and considering I live in West Palm Beach, we could go golfing and sign the franchise agreement at the same time. I love West Palm Beach because it's a wealthy city. The rich love to spend time here. After playing our round of golf, we could visit the Flagler Museum. Also known as Whitehall, Henry Flagler's house is so huge it's a truly awe-inspiring experience to visit. And when I am there, I feel right at home.

Above all others, Flagler is my idol. I know he is no longer with us, but in all honesty, I carry a living memory of his example in my heart. I have very high esteem for those with the courage to realize their dreams, as I do. I consider myself a member of the Achiever Family. I hope to welcome you into our family soon, and have no fear – Henry Flagler will be watching over us all from above taking care of us from the sky. The fact that I live in the same city Flagler did is no coincidence. I will try my best to achieve as much as he did. This business opportunity may make a lot of sense for you. It's simple: you pay a one-time franchise fee, and in return, gain the exclusive privilege to use and sell Diamond Heads products for a period of 20 years. Among the better aspects of owning a Diamond Heads franchise, consider the passive-sales side. If someone who lives in your territory orders a product online, that purchase will be considered part of your sales, even though you did nothing special to seal the deal. Here's an example: Joe lives in downtown London and orders the new luxury gold ring online. We receive the order and ship the item directly to Joe's home. You wisely purchased the England master franchise two years back. Because Joe lives your territory, you receive a commission. This is called a natural business sale. You didn't exactly have to break a sweat to make it happen. However, the sale will partly be due to the hard work you've poured into great marketing, ensuring everyone in England knows the Diamond Heads brand. All the while, the official Diamond Heads website will generate easy sales for you. The price of a master franchise varies from state to state and from country to country.

The only territory that will never be available for sale is Hawaii, which is easily understood: Hawaii is the reason Diamond Heads exists today. Our mission is to reflect and capture the beauty of Hawaii through our high-end quality products. We will always promote this magical island on a global scale, because this is where Diamond Heads was born – and "Born in the USA" is essential to our DNA. This is the only place in the world where a stunning ocean-side and a paradise called Waikiki Beach can coexist. Imagine surfing right after your day shift at Diamond Heads… If you currently live somewhere in America where the economy is sluggish and the unemployment rate is high, then consider booking a flight to Hawaii, with your mind firmly set on making this a one-way trip. The climate in Hawaii is a tropical one but the humidity tends to be a bit less extreme due to constant trade winds from the east. The rainy season is from October to April. Year-round temperatures range between 67 and 88 degrees Fahrenheit. At this point, I would like to offer a special gift to all my readers. The next time you visit us, remember to take a 15% discount off all Diamond Heads products available for purchase. Items must be ordered through our official website at www.diamondheads.co by entering the promo code *billionaire*. You will notice that we have selected black diamonds to adorn almost all of our products. Black diamonds are intended to reflect and relate back to the color of volcanic rock. Black diamonds are an expression of our roots. Of course, in future, we may also produce a limited-edition range of products using the pink Canadian Diamond, called the Canadian Limited Edition.

Wow, this combination of writing and generating million dollar ideas is cool, on every level. You're doing a great job Dan – I'm proud of you (sometimes, we must take the time to offer ourselves this kind of motivational praise). I hope this sales pitch has been effective in convincing you to climb on board with us. A long time ago, I learned that leaders tend to attract leaders. Every day, I do my best to remember that. It's hard for me to bring this chapter to an end. I love to talk about Diamond Heads because I am passionate about this challenge and my drive is almost limitless. Think of the way a mother glowingly describes her child – that is the way I feel about Diamond Heads. Believe me, you'll be tire of hearing about it before I'll be tire of telling the story. However, I *will* close this chapter, and do so by sharing my latest thoughts on our products lines. A while ago, people began telling us that our logo was terrific and would look perfect on a high-end fashion line. What do you think? Frankly, we weren't expecting that, but of course, we're delighted to hear it. Great things can happen in life, right out of nowhere. And who knows – perhaps you're a fashion specialist who can help design and market high-end clothing… in which case, by all means, we want to hear from you. We also received commentary about establishing an exclusive line of products for women. We might call this line Diamond Heads For Her. Again, feel free to add your own feedback; brilliant ideas almost always come from thinking outside the box.

Please take the same approach when dealing with your own business project. Ask for outside feedback and people will almost always offer it to help you achieve your goal. Needless to say, you must always copyright your ideas in advance to avoid intellectual property theft. Moreover, carefully choose the people with whom you will share your ideas. There will always be those who destroy your dreams in the name of trying to protect you. They do not actually protect you. They are simply jealous people who resent you because you want more from life, and seek to slow your progress on the road to success.

Diamond Heads was a weak and vulnerable idea at first. If I had chosen to share the project with the wrong people, this chapter would not exist. Instead, I carefully chose the people in whom I confided, and my confidence rose quickly. Choosing the right business partner is also critical. If you join weak partners, you will naturally end up with weak results. Guillaume is and has been the right partner all along because he knows exactly what he is doing. I am not a jewelry specialist, but partnering with the right person has hugely increased my chances of success. The most beautiful thing about our partnership is I couldn't have built Diamond Heads without Guillaume, and Guillaume couldn't have built Diamond Heads without me. Now that is the perfect win-win deal. In my previous book, I stated that I because of my father's horrible experience, I would not partner with anyone other than my wife. I have since changed my mind. I realized that forming partnerships with the world's most driven people is a slam-dunk. As I wrote previously, this book was about business opportunities, and the good news is we are far from finished. In fact, the word *finished* must be eliminated from your vocabulary. We have known one another for several chapters now. I consider myself to be a boundlessly ambitious achiever, and my goal is to attract you into my world.

Again, if you feel this is not for you, you can bail out at any time. I know from experience that it's hard to leave your comfort zone. I would like to say that's not true of me, but I remember my roots, too. Back in the '90s, I was in school like everyone else – and I did not like school at all. I felt like a caged tiger the entire time.

Except on Fridays...The perfect song for this chapter is: Diamonds, by Rihanna. "Shine bright like a diamond..." As you can tell, I love diamonds. Then again, doesn't everybody?

LOVE AND YOUR BELIEFS

I will kick off this chapter a little bit differently by sharing the perfect song from the outset: Love Changes Everything, by Climie Fisher.

In your life, are you a loved person? I sincerely hope you have someone special to share your everyday moments, kids to cherish and watch grow up, parents who are proud of you, friends who love coming over for dinner, pets that unconditionally love and treat you like the best person in the world. What is the connection between love and a book on becoming a billionaire? Well, love is the very first human need, after food and water. When we feel we are loved on a daily basis, anything becomes possible. If you are financially wealthy but have nobody who loves you, then – sorry to say – you are probably the poorest person in the world. Nothing can buy or replace love. On the other hand, if your family and friends love you immensely, you are part of a lucky club and can consider yourself very rich indeed. I like money because it allows me to travel, visit incredible places and meet amazing people. But make no mistake: above all, I want to be loved. My heart beats in harmony with my wife, Chantal, who is absolutely the best possible partner for me. She's always there for me and almost always supports my crazy ideas. My wife is genuinely happy to see me when I come home – and what could be better than that? My best friends today are still the ones I met in school 25 years ago. We get together for dinner parties once or twice a year, and always have a blast. These people don't care about my money. They're around me for something much more important: true friendship. My son Vincent is the most beautiful and intelligent kid I could ever have imagined. He is a source of great joy and happy memories, and of course, I love him beyond all measure. It's no coincidence that we've been to Walt Disney World seven times. Naturally, being my son, he dreams of owning my Tim Hortons restaurant when he grows up. Believe me, I am the luckiest dad in the world. I could not ask for any better lot in life. In your life, can you count on your loved ones to help you achieve your future business projects? Everything is so much easier when a loving partner supports you.

In business, you must re-invest all the love you have received in your life. People will notice it in everything you do, and your actions will be rewarded. Think about it: Love and passion are powerful, yet also invisible. If you want to make money but are willing to give back very little love in return, your results will be disappointing indeed. Listen to your favorite song and feel how much love radiates from it. That's what makes it so great. We were born of love, and every time I witness a great work of art, I see the love that went into creating it. You must absolutely see the world from a loving standpoint. Most people see the world as a scary place filled with violence. I see it from another perspective, by choice. Every day, I try to show love in everything I do. If you're ever in Orlando, Florida, do yourself a favor and set aside some time to visit Charley's Steak House. You will be surprised by the love they put into every operational detail. The food they offer is as amazing as the quality of service. From the moment you pass through those huge doors, you will be treated to the delicious aroma of steak – and also, the sweet smell of success. They are proud to be recognized as one of America's Top Ten Steak Houses. They also love to point out that a number of U.S. Presidents have dined there. If I had one day left to live, I would like to spend it there with my family and loved ones. After a wonderful meal, I would feel happy, grateful and at peace. Try to duplicate the level of execution at Charley's in your own business, putting lots of love into everything you do, and there's no doubt success will be waiting for you. Nothing is impossible for the power of Love, no matter who or what or where you are in life.

You can be whoever you want and have whatever you want if you use it properly. People who have built large fortunes always talk about the things they love; you will never hear them reminiscing about the past. They know how amazing their lives can be today and tomorrow by sending their energy in the right direction. Just think of how much Henry Ford went on about his black Model T. Draw up an inventory of everything you love. Your job consists of doing things you love as much as possible every day. Can you be engaged in doing what you love most of the time? Now, I know – not everyone gets to spend every day on the golf course… but can you double or triple the time you spend exclusively on the items in your inventory list? Life is much easier than we think it is. Once you begin to understand this, the evidence begins to appear everywhere.

Six years ago, I had a very different belief system. I thought Life was difficult, that having very little time left to do the things I love was a perfectly normal state of affairs. I only believed this nonsense because it's what people had been telling me since I was a kid. And so I internalized it, believing it must all be true, since everybody repeated the same mantra over and over. I was making tons of money, but my life was a grind of long and exhausting working hours. If I played a measly 10 rounds of golf in a year, that was a great year. Business troubles were the norm, and it seemed like every new day dawned with its own new problem at my Tim Hortons store. One day, I told myself: Life should be easy. Enjoying my wealth should be the norm, not the exception. I must do what I love to do much more often. That was the day I trashed my old belief system for good. My problems did not all disappear in 24 hours, but I saw new possible solutions. The solutions had always been there; I just hadn't been able to see them.

The following summer, I played 25 rounds of golf. I've never played fewer in any summer since. My former grinding 55-hour workweek now averages more like 15. I achieved these results the very first year I changed my belief system. My bottom line (profits) doubled. My new belief system was not only more relaxing, it was also more rewarding on the financial side. It was the best of both worlds, and I was suddenly living in paradise. And I am still living there today.

Do you have a negative belief system like the one I carried with me for too many years? Identify and write these beliefs down. These worthless beliefs impede you every day and prevent you from doing the things you love the most. Do you think the world is full of bad people? I did, a decade ago. I transformed that to: great people are always there to help me in everything I do. I read inspiring books for the great stories they hold, proof that the world is filled with great productive, accomplished. TV news programs do not reflect or intersect with this belief, so I avoid them. People in other countries around the world are fast to say negative things about Americans. That's the worst nonsense I've ever heard. I've traveled through almost all 50 states and I can assure every reader that those comments are simply dead wrong. Americans are the warmest, most helpful and generous people on the planet. Furthermore, they are positive achievers, always believing that great things lie ahead. I have a deep appreciation for that Think Big attitude. If you hold negative beliefs that prevent you from being a happy and loving person, you are right. If you hold empowering beliefs that will help you achieve anything you desire, then you are right, too. Taking my life as an example, I was right in both ways of thinking… but I prefer my new life and beliefs.

Do you believe that becoming a billionaire is inappropriate or impossible? I believe I can become a billionaire. I also believe I can become one without harming anyone. I believe I can become one without making anyone poorer. I believe I can become one and remain humble. And I believe I can change the world for the better by becoming a billionaire. As you can see, my beliefs are constructive. They are in line with where I want to go. If you want to be rich but simultaneously believe that money is bad in itself, and inappropriate for you, then you are headed in the wrong direction. Examine your beliefs for evidence that you have mistakenly absorbed what everybody always tells us is true. You may have heard this garbage before: "Money doesn't grow on trees." Of course it doesn't grow on trees – but the old phrase really means that money is scarce and rare. This is not true: money is as plentiful as water on earth. You must change this belief as fast as you can. Believe it or not, my mother repeated that line over and over to me when I was a kid, and I mistakenly took it to heart. After all, my mother could only be telling me the truth, right? Nevertheless, I changed that belief when I decided to jump into the business world. I knew the good life was out there waiting for me, while my weekly paycheck was far from satisfying. Another perfect song for this chapter is: Break Your Plans, by The Fray. Break your old belief system and create a new one that will perfectly suit your goals and desires.

You will probably still hear the bad old beliefs coming at you from others again and again. I don't argue with anyone who spouts negative thoughts. I know we are all different, and at different places in our lives. Nowadays, I laugh to myself whenever I hear someone uttering negative, destructive beliefs. I realize the person knows absolutely nothing. At the same time, of course, I can't blame that person. He's simply repeating what everyone has heard over and over and, after all, we tend to learn by repetition. So now you know. You have no reason to leave your negative beliefs as they are. By changing them, as I did six years ago, you will have more time to do the things you really love. Do you like your job or the business you're in? Fifteen years ago, I was not happy or fulfilled by my level of achievement. I knew deep down that I was capable of far more. You will have to ask yourself real questions if you want to do the things you love on a full-time basis. I know you have bills to pay – we all do. I have tons of bills to pay. But remember, you weren't put on this Earth just to pay bills. You original plan was much greater than that, and you will only be satisfied when you feel you are on track and achieving your original plan. The race of our lives began in the very first instant, when each of us won a competition with millions of other spermatozoids. Each of us made it first to the egg. That, elementally, explains why we are happy when we feel like we are winning in life. We are winners in every one of our trillions of cells, right from the very beginning. You have an opportunity here to change what is not yet perfect. I strongly encourage you to take that introspection test and correct what does not work. You will be rewarded on a grand scale. You have the power within you to do this, so do this for yourself. Life should be a fun, amazing experience. Let the magic of your life begin. Your dreams and your reality can be much closer together than you think.

YOUR LINKEDIN PAGE OF THE FUTURE

I won't spend too much time discussing Facebook, because frankly, I think people waste far too much time on the site. If you are making money through Facebook, then congratulations, and keep up the good work. But in most cases, I simply don't understand why the hell people are on there. You should always think about your return on time invested. My guess is the average Facebook user receives a very low return. The great news is that you can delete your Facebook profile (it's less difficult than it used to be), which is exactly what I did last year. I was sick and tired of the site. I mean, Facebook is a great business for its founder and CEO Mark Zuckerberg, but I doubt if it's of any real use to you.

On the other hand, LinkedIn is a really useful online resource, a great destination to meet the achievers of the world. If you send me a LinkedIn invitation, I will gladly accept it and consult your profile to look over your career and/or business path. Yes, I agree: once you're in the general LinkedIn pack, it's hard to differentiate yourself, to stand out. Nevertheless, this is the place where I meet the geniuses of social networking. Their ideas are so innovative that you have to sign a disclaimer notice from the start, which they proudly call **industrial secret protection.** I am in the process of working with them right now, which means we are covered by such a disclaimer, but stay tuned, I will give you updates on our results in due course. I know people who have successfully closed business deals on LinkedIn, but I would say this social media platform is best suited to initiating contacts. I may be wrong, but I've heard that a new sales deal is usually only closed after 5 follow-through contacts. After that, repeat and referral business comes more easily.

Last month I made what we might call a quantum leap. I thought: let's put the Law of Attraction to maximum use. I projected myself into the future, as though all my goals were part of my daily reality. It was a really enjoyable and empowering exercise. Your mind doesn't know it has been projected into the future, instead believing that this is your reality, right now. I like this exercise because it's a way of telling the world: this is where I want to go. In a sense, you are committing yourself to a goal.

Of course, some people will say you are just lying to yourself. Never mind – I would immediately tell those negative people that this is my LinkedIn page of the future – and best of all, it's available for consultation today. I enjoy engaging in that kind of new visualization experience. Life should be fun, don't you think? That's why I love Hawaii so much; it's my idea of the perfect playground. Tell me: what does your future look like? Do you see yourself as the best real estate agent in the city? The days ahead are yours to design, any way you want. If your inner voice constantly tells you that a lack of money will prevent you from becoming the person you want to be, then I can see your future very clearly: difficult. Here is what people with great ambitions and no money do: they find sweet spots of opportunity where they can create value and then sell their unique expertise or form business partnerships with the world's wealthy people. Then they work like mad until success manifests itself. When you visit LinkedIn, you will discover a multitude of successful people. Ask them questions and about 90% of the time, they will gladly respond. There's no need to be afraid – from my side, I can't recall ever refusing to answer someone who sent me a message. People with experience in achieving success love to share that information, and above all, love to see others succeed as well. Do you like to cold call? Nobody does. However, I know one high-achieving insurance agent with the rare discipline to make 200 cold calls every day. Out of those, he knows he will probably generate two new customers per day… at best. He is rich because he does something special nobody else is willing to do. You see, if you really want to achieve great things, you must eliminate shyness from your behavioral set. You have to go out and get your well-deserved piece of the pie.

LinkedIn will help you do this, and if you have the courage to imagine your LinkedIn page of the future, your will generate results and make success a reality more quickly than you might have imagined. The special theme song for this chapter is: We Go Home, by Adam Cohen. Yes, we heading Home, because we know what our future is made of. We are literally creating it.

A FOLLOW-UP ON MY GOALS

It's human nature to be curious, and almost everyone is curious about the life of a writer. Many books are generally entertaining and even helpful, but have you ever noticed that when you finish reading, you can't be absolutely certain that the author is as successful as he claimed to be? Your suspicions are warranted, because often, no clear details are given. As you have read in previous chapters, I stated this book would be different.

To satisfy your curiosity, here's an update on my life. At the end of my first book, I wrote down my list of goals for the future. That was in 2012; we are now entering 2015. Three years is a short time, but let's check on the list, and the progress:

Launch my own foundation no later than 2015.

I have set the mission of the foundation, and will launch it as planned in the fall of 2015. I will offer further details later in the book.

Create two new online businesses no later than 2018.

Diamond Heads is the first of those businesses:
www.diamondheads.co

The second is the official website for this book
www.billionairerightnextdoor.com

And yes, it feels great to be three years ahead of schedule.

Create or acquire three new businesses no later than 2020.

The first of these is Diamond Heads. The second is a new business called Credit Help, specializing in small loans, or microloans if you prefer. This brand-new business was born just one month ago. We are still riding the learning curve with Credit Help, but we will succeed. My third new business is Tremblay World, established to manage the book website, lectures and books sales as a whole. Tremblay Holdings is a more mature company that manages a real estate investment portfolio. To date, we are proud to be invested in six U.S. states. When I wrote my first book, I was already the owner of my 2 Tim Hortons franchises, so those don't count as "new."

Own 1000 real estate properties no later than 2025.

One of the songs I love to sing is Time Is On My Side. In all honesty, I am far from achieving this enormous goal. We are currently involved in 20 investment properties in the U.S. and Canada. But stay tuned, because we will definitely succeed.

Create a hotel chain, with no timeframe specified.

I may have made a mistake here by not specifying a timeframe, but for now, my focus is elsewhere than the hotel business. However, I never say never: a great deal can arise at a moment's notice.

Launch my first IPO on the NYSE no later than 2030.

I plan to launch Diamond Heads on the stock market within the next 5 years.

Organize a millionaires' Caribbean cruise, with no timeframe specified.

I would love to organize this kind of event sometime between now and 2016, but it will all depend on timing and how things evolve. You can send me your confirmation if you want to reserve a spot on board, and we can thereby gauge the general interest level.

Become a worldwide speaker no later than 2020.

Since writing and publishing my first book, I have given 5 separate lectures and greatly enjoyed them. However, I'm not looking to make a living from speaking engagements – it's something I do because I love to interact with ambitious, enthusiastic people. I was serious when I wrote that I would do it all for free; unfortunately, my business also needs me and takes up a lot of my time. I will continue to accept speaking engagements when I'm invited, and hope to see you at one of them.

Develop a global brand no later than 2025.

Well, instead of one, why not go for two? Diamond Heads and Tremblay World are the two next worldwide brands that will be on everyone's lips.

Own a private jet no later than 2032.

Rest assured, I will have my jet well before that date, not out of any burning desire, but due to simple travel necessity.

That's the end of my list. Am I worried about whether or not I can accomplish all of these massive goals? Well, yes and no. Frankly, I won't try to do it all by myself. I will need your help. Where do you see yourself in my organization? Could you be a team member exploring real estate markets and closing deals for Tremblay Holdings? Would you prefer to organize annual events for Tremblay World? I am sure I can find a spot where you will be at your best. Ask and you shall receive...

The best thing about setting major goals like these is that it's not your job to know all the details about how everything will happen. Have no fear, the universe itself will do most of the work for you. The only thing you need to clearly know is your desire. If things do not go as planned, then you will know the project is not well suited to you. Most of us know of the Law of Attraction operating in the universe. Sadly enough, only 2% use it. How can this be? It may seem incredible, but I conclude that the majority of people shy away from seeking money and the great lifestyle that comes with it. They are afraid of it because it is represents the Unknown. Are you ready for the next chapter? I hope you are still with me, wide-awake and full of energy. If not, please put the book down and relax for a moment. You and your mind deserve a break. Let your mind set your ideas in order; after all, it is at work even while you sleep. Everything is under control, and the fact of your presence here right now, reading this book, is no mere coincidence. You were meant to be here.

THE ANNUAL DIAMOND HEADS MASTERMIND EVENT IN HAWAII

If you have reached this chapter, you must be cranked, pumped and fired up. Your leadership level must be dialed to the max and you're ready to reach for the stars. Don't worry, I will immediately request that our pilot plot a course for them, as long as we don't risk running out of fuel!

In all seriousness, I have something truly great to share with you. Diamond Heads will host a world-class event called Mastermind in Hawaii in the fall of 2015 and in the successive years to come. This seminar event will be managed and organized by Karine Lefebvre. Who is Karine? I would simply describe her as the most accomplished sales woman I have ever met. Conjure up the most difficult sales scenario imaginable, and Karine is guaranteed to close it. I challenge you to challenge Karine and you will understand what I mean. Our goal in the first year is to sign up a limited number of 100 participants from all over the world, then build the event for future editions. If you're thinking of joining us, I can promise that you will have the blast of your life. We'll invite six renowned business founders who will appear exclusively at our event. I will be among the speakers and available anytime if you want to speak to me in person. We'll be sharing up-to-date cutting-edge information at the seminar. I think a total business immersion experience is an excellent way to learn how to conduct business and profit from available opportunities. As when you are learning a new language, total immersion works faster and more efficiently than anything else. In fall 2015, we will host this first annual business event sponsored by Diamond Heads in Honolulu, Hawaii. If you dream of visiting or re-visiting this magical island of endless possibilities, and also want to start your own company, then consider this the ideal way to accomplish both goals at once.

This kind of event may or may not be for you, but you are nevertheless welcome to join our group and give it a shot. Over the course of two straight days, we will present the opportunities available in current markets. You will have a chance to hear six U.S. business experts share their knowledge, experience and expertise. Our team will also take the time to review your business plan and guide you through the process.

If you're thinking of upgrading your skills and exploring what's available, you must consider this offer. We want you to break free from your internal limitations and fears. After all, this event is all about you. We guarantee your satisfaction. For registration and further details please visit: www.billionairerightnextdoor.com The sales pitch is finally over. But in all honesty, I don't consider it a sales pitch, rather a description and invitation to a great win-win event for all. As you know, I've been successful in business for the past 14 years. It's now time to work seriously on your own path to success. Reading books on the subject is a great way to start, but ultimately that is not enough. I did not build up my own success solely by reading books. In fact, I participated in five separate seminars over the years. Every one of them left me with something new to apply in my daily routine. I also made friends and contacts I am still using today. As I recall, one of them was held in Toronto, Canada in the fall of 2009, a full two-day event focused on investing in real estate. The energy level was amazing. At the same time, I must admit not all of the seminar content was for me. I was already a multimillionaire at the time. Still, this convention was the spark I needed to realize that I had to break free, get focused and start building my American real estate portfolio. Soon after the seminar, I was acquiring my first building in Orlando, Florida. It was the first piece of real estate for my corporation, Tremblay Holdings. The rest is history, but you get the point: seminars and conferences are great because of the immersion effect and the high energy level.

The next seminar that provided me with a huge payoff afterwards was in 2010, in Orlando, at the Walt Disney World resort. I love Walt Disney's legendary phrase, "It all started with a mouse." My phrase would be "It all started with the first guest in my Tims store on February 4, 2001." It was a two-day seminar designed for Tim Hortons owners. Once again, it was great thanks to the immersion process, which allows you to think outside the box and discover the opportunities available in your day-to-day business affairs. During the seminar, I discovered that my restaurants were strong on the speed-of-service side but weak on quality training for new team members.

Employee turnover can be costly, and your business can lose big if you don't do things properly. When new members join the team, they make the normal mistakes that are part of the learning process. Your guest service suffers when food orders are mishandled. I realized that improved training would mean less turnover for us, fewer mistakes, better service, and more sales. And in the final analysis, a better bottom line. When I returned, I initiated a training review process with all my managers. The benefits were swift in coming. Overall sales per year for our two stores have jumped by $500,000 since the Orlando seminar. I wouldn't say it was the only reason behind the change, but probably the primary and main one. The perfect song for this chapter is: Learning To Fly, by Pink Floyd. Seminars will help you learn to fly. I prefer seminars to conferences because the immersive timeframe is greater and more intense. The average conference lasts 90 minutes to two hours. Seminars usually run for two days. Seminars will bring you much better results faster.

FOUNDATION

Earlier in the book, I mentioned that I would discuss my foundation, which will become operational in 2015. It also lays out an intriguing and profitable opportunity for you, on a number of levels. As I've written, my long-term goal is to see people succeed, and the goal of my foundation is to help people achieve their literary dreams. Every year, my foundation will host a global literary contest, providing a First Prize of $100,000 in cash.

Have you ever dreamt of writing your own book? Have you, in fact, already written one? The contest rules are simple: you must own the rights to your book, meaning it must be free and clear of any publishing contracts. On our side, we commit ourselves to using all books submitted for contest purposes only. The subject of your book must fall into one of the following categories: success biographies, self-help, health and/or lifestyle trends. No other subjects will be eligible. Your book must be 40,000 words long or more, and have been previously edited. It must be in English only. No other languages will be eligible. I will be one of the five judges on board for the selection process. If you would like to be one of our judges, please send us your application, and note that the position is on a voluntary basis. Of course, even working as a volunteer, you will be part of the Tremblay World team. To be selected as a judge, you obviously must love to read, have time available and be highly credible. Remember, you will be representing the Tremblay brand organization. Our goal is to become the world reference in literary contests. And as a writer, just imagine what you could do with that $100,000 cash prize. I hope that potential award will be tantalizing enough to lure you from your comfort zone and enter the competition. Imagine the impact of being the first winner of a global contest. Victory could lead to publishing interest and a real chance at a serious literary contract. In fact, the publisher of my own book would probably be the first to approach you with a deal. Furthermore, publishing on a scale this large would almost certainly bring you invitations to seminars and interviews. We would be the first to invite you to our annual Diamond Heads seminar in Hawaii to celebrate your success. You would be invited to take the stage in front of our audience and speak about your experience and how you accomplished your goal. Believe me, it's like being a rock star. I speak from experience, as that was the case with my first book release. Afterwards, people will suddenly look at you and speak to you in a very different manner. The winner will also be awarded the official contest trophy in front of our group in Hawaii. You must intend to share your unique experiences with the reading community, and have your book contribute something new and productive.

We hope and expect to generate significant interest in the contest, to stimulate creativity around the world and contribute to emerging success stories. Once again, we are in a perfect win-win scenario. To submit your own book, please visit the official website for the one you are currently reading: www.billionairerightnextdoor.com If you are not a natural writer, this contest opportunity may not be for you. However, I would advise you to carefully consider the project. I never knew I could write a book until I actually wrote Page One as a test run. As you may have noticed, I am not Shakespeare; after all, I am first and foremost a businessman. Despite that, my books are bestsellers, and that's more than enough for me. So follow my example. At first, the task will be difficult, because doing something new rarely feels natural. It took me four months to write my first book; this one will take three weeks. I'm not boasting here – I just want to illustrate how things evolve. The more you write, the better you write. It's just like everything else in life, isn't it?

I know you can successfully meet this challenge. At the very least, you can give it a try. This is an immediate opportunity to win; and best of all, you would make your own important contribution to the contest, so it's really win-win. One very useful tool I use while writing is to set out daily goals. My goal during the writing of this book was to reach 2000 words a day during the week, which took up about 3 hours of my time. Not the end of the world, right? On weekends, the goal was reduced to 1000 words. Never forget your family – they are more important than anything else. I have no minimum word requirement for this book, for the simple reason that I neither want to waste my time, nor yours. When I feel that I have given the best I have to help you succeed, I will type The End. After this book, I will take a break from writing until the time comes to help you reach the next level. In the past, a number of writers told me that a typical book must respect various rules for the number of chapters, length, and even structure. I will never follow rules set out by others because I never achieved success in the past by following pre-established rules. I prefer to rewrite the established rules and improve them. Many years ago, the Tim Hortons organization taught and trained me to be daring and different, and that is what I do every day, in everything. Participation in the contest is free of charge. I conceived of it one Saturday morning in September 2014 because making a contribution to a good cause is the most fulfilling feeling in life.

The perfect song for this chapter is: Begin Again, by Taylor Swift.

WHAT IF...?

What if you could have all the time you wanted to do what you really enjoy? What if that goal could be on your mid-term time horizon? What if you could have a private chef at home preparing all your meals and lunch for the kids? What if you could travel the world on a cruise for an entire year and visit all the beautiful spots on our planet?

Is this your scenario for your future, or just a mere wish? If you knew right now that you could make millions of dollars, but you'd have to stop what you're currently doing day-to-day and act differently, would you do so immediately? I'm guessing you answered *yes* in a split-second but that as you read on, that answer turned into *but I can't do that*. Do you know how I know? The exact same thing happened to me every time I began to think about propelling my life to the next level. I still remember the key moment very well, when I started my Tim Hortons franchise purchase deal 14 years ago. All the papers had been signed, but we were waiting for the completion of construction. Every day, I would visit the construction site to see how things were evolving. On site, I would imagine my life as a business owner, and the kind of relationship I would have with my future team members. I felt like I was making a huge quantum leap in my life. I looked at this new chapter as a mountain of challenges. I felt a hectic mix of excitement and fear of the unknown. The climb ahead was undeniably steep, but humans are unbelievably adaptive creatures. If you asked me the same question today, I'd say that managing my stores is sometimes challenging, but I am used to it. I call this the cost of doing business. Running a business is like playing with a jack-in-the-box. One minute the music is playing perfectly, but you know that the clown can explode out of the box at any time.

You are probably at that phase in your life when you are keen to explore new opportunities. Keep in mind that in the beginning, the process will be no different for you than it was for me or anyone else who preceded you. You must be prepared for discomfort at first, which eventually gives way in the mid- to long-term to the reward of cherishing your accomplishments and milestones. What if your desire for success and wealth were more powerful than anything else? Life has a great tendency to reward people with a clear vision of what they want. When people today are unable to describe where they want to be 10 years from now, I have a ready answer for where they will end up: exactly where they are right now, if not further behind.

I consider myself to be a very kind and gentle person, but at the same time, I can't stand mediocrity and incompetence. Over the years, I've fired many, many employees who where slacking on the job. My answer is always the same: it's no harder to be a superstar team member than it is to be a slacker. It takes virtually the same amount of energy, except the former takes pride every day in achieving his absolute best. However, I've never seen a slacker on the job who was proud of his mediocrity. The best advice I can offer a future business owner is to praise your good employees while simultaneously firing the people I would call "business destroyers." Go ahead and play the "What If" game. It's enjoyable, and your mind will begin to see these possibilities as perfectly doable. You must, of course, be aware of your inner negative voice. *It will never happen* is what you will hear. The good news is, you are neither an alien nor a born failure if you hear that voice in your head. I have that inner voice, as do others. I am no different from you. The day you understand this will be the day you know: if he can do it, I can too.

The spark that inspired me to start writing my first book came two years earlier. I was reading a bestselling book by a relatively ordinary person who probably hadn't achieved 2% of what I already had. I clearly remember wondering: exactly what is blocking me from starting my first book? If this person can write a bestselling book, then so can I. From that very moment, all my mental blocks disappeared. Sometimes, frustration itself has this special power to destroy our blocks. When I reach a certain level of frustration, there is a point when I say to myself: that's enough, something has to change. My greatest moments of frustration have often been the spark igniting me to achieve more and aim for a better life. Now that you know that we are exactly the same deep down inside, can we achieve things together? I hope all your blocks have now been removed and relegated to the past. Tell your mind to forget about them and move on. I know it's not that simple, but for now let's move forward and look ahead rather than behind. The sky is clear and bright and nothing can stop us. We are already zooming along in our jet, but wait: let's ask the pilot if he can flip on the turbocharger. With all our blocks removed, our jet plane is much lighter, and who knows, maybe we can hit Mach 2. The perfect song for this chapter is: This Is How We Do, by Katy Perry. It's impossible for me to hear this song without feeling a strong inner drive to achieve.

ONE-ON-ONE MASTERMIND DAY AT DIAMOND HEAD, HAWAII

If you really want to turbocharge your life and reach the soaring speed of our jet plane, consider an invitation to join me in Hawaii for a daylong one-on-one business session. We call it the Mastermind Day at Diamond Head in Hawaii.

If you need personal mentorship, this could be the perfect journey for you. Simply make your reservation for a specific date and I will pick you up at Honolulu International Airport in our new Tesla. Since this is your special day, I will hand you the keys so you can give her a spin. After all, the entire day will be dedicated to driving your life to the next level. If you like, our first destination will be the famed Diamond Head volcano itself. Since we won't want to waste any of your precious time while driving, you can then tell me your entire story – where you're from, your past experiences and, most importantly, where you want to go in your life.

Arriving at our destination, you can decide if we should climb to the very top or stay below and begin our busy working day – a day spent working on your plan. If you ask me, I would suggest that we take the time to climb and admire this wonder of nature. Of course, the final decisions on your special day are all yours. The volcano is extremely important to us because this is where it all began for our corporation, Diamond Heads International. We believe the volcano has an elemental energy that can make all your dreams come true. The Walt Disney World slogan is "Where dreams come true." I think the Diamond Heads slogan is slightly different: Where ideas of wealth begin. Food and drink will be plentiful throughout, as our staff members plan out every single detail. We pride ourselves on our leadership values and top-flight performance when it comes to satisfaction. Believe me, you will feel like the most important person in the world – because after all, you are. Our goal will be to pave your way to success. Since you are the only guest today, the focus will be entirely on you, making it easier for us to evaluate and analyze your special needs and dreams. Hawaii is the most magical place on Earth when it comes to pulling the plug and still remaining focused enough to work on a plan. As our guest, you can also visit the Diamonds Heads world headquarters facility. We will explain how we manage and grow the business worldwide, and introduce you to our corporate team.

If you're a fan of a massage, the choice is yours: any type suited to your needs, since it would be great to kick off the second part of the day in relaxed form. We will still have some work to do and a lot of things to discuss, but don't you think it would be better to do it in a more laid-back mode? A clear mind tends to make better business decisions. For lunch, we offer a diversified menu, since we know people don't want to eat health food all the time. Given the exotic locale, we strongly advise our guest to choose an island specialty to enjoy the Hawaiian experience to the max. From there, the guest decides what type of action he prefers for the rest of his Mastermind Day. Golfing, beach time, mountain climbing, snorkeling, catamaran, ocean fishing, Sea-Doo… you name it! The goal is to continue the work while adding in play at the same time.

For dinner, our team will join us for a meal at the best restaurant in town. We love the place because of the exotic after-dinner Hawaiian dancing show. In the closing review, we will provide you with a final copy of the customized Mastermind plan for your life, along with souvenir photos taken throughout your magical day. These Mastermind experiences in paradise are utterly unique. I created them because I enjoy feeling that I am making a contribution and a genuine difference in someone's life. I hope you will consider this exclusive offer. For more details please visit our official web site at www.billionairerightnextdoor.com Mastermind experiences in Hawaii are not available every day all year 'round, because as you already know, my wife and I split our time between Honolulu, West Palm Beach and Montreal. Now you understand why I have to consider procuring a private jet at some point in the future. The One-on-One Mastermind is a total immersion experience that removes you from your daily routine and allows you to suddenly realize that all the possibilities are right there in front of you, available and doable. As you return to your hotel or the airport, we will hand you an official certificate documenting your One-on-One Mastermind day at Diamond Head.

This certificate also doubles as your passport to join the next High Achievers Society trip, with more details on that coming later in the book. In addition, our team will provide follow-through as needed until you have accomplished your plan and made it a part of your daily reality. Our goal is to maximize the return on your time invested in Hawaii. The perfect song for this chapter is Hey Soul Sister by the band Train, for an obvious reason: you can hear ukulele on the backbeat throughout the song.

CHANGING THE WORLD TOGETHER

This chapter is about sharing our thoughts on a different issue. Your opportunity here is focused more on doing something good, and feeling good by doing so. I sincerely hope that you don't simply dream of making money for solely selfish reasons. If so, you will feel empty if you end up wealthy but have done nothing that will last. What legacy will you leave behind after your time on Earth? It's entirely appropriate and lovely to say "my children and grandchildren"… but what else will be on your list?

I do not think we need to act on a major scale to spark a massive chain reaction. In 1880, America's Standard Oil Company was owned by John D. Rockefeller. A worldwide banking crisis had recently ended, with Mr. Rockefeller being the man who most benefited from the crisis. He not only bought almost all of his competitors across the country, he also bought the complete vertical chain (suppliers, transport, delivery and retailers). After those massive-scale acquisitions, he became so powerful he could fix his own prices. Imagine a man so powerful he could rule politics and dictate anything he wanted. In 1888, John D. Rockefeller became the first billionaire in the world. Imagine what a billion could buy at that time! He and his best friend, J.P. Morgan, controlled a huge part of the U.S. economy and there was very little politicians could do to stop them. If you're looking for the true masters of the country, look no further than these men who established massive trusts and monopolies. In 1911, the U.S. government broke up the Standard Oil trust into a series of companies like Exxon and Chevron, but guess who mainly remained in control of these new entities? That's correct – our friend Rockefeller.

This cartel has dominated the economy for decades and decades and ruled our lives into the present day, but the good news is that this era is coming to an end. Dictators around the world always fall eventually; some stay in power for decades, but the final results are always the same. You and I have the real power in our hands today because we can choose what we buy. When you buy a product, you are voting for that company.

I am very proud of my parents, because two years ago, they bought a Chevrolet Volt, the official GM electric car. When my father showed me the car, he told me that it would be his personal contribution to the environment in his lifetime. He has gone on to completely switch all his gas-powered tools to electric ones: electric lawnmower, tree-trimmer, you name it – if it's electric, my father's got it. Now you may think this is nothing but a drop in the ocean when compared to petroleum magnates. I agree… but then again, that ocean will no longer belong to those oil barons. For one thing, my father has convinced me to change my viewpoint, act upon it and therefore follow his example.

In 2015, I will buy my first Tesla, the bold new 100% electric sports car. When my Volvo SUV dies, I will replace it with another SUV, also by Tesla. Boom! No more gasoline engines in my life. And not only will I never go back to gasoline, I will convince as many people as I can to do the same. But that's just for starters. In 2015, I will also cover my roof with solar panels. After all, we get a lot of sun in West Palm Beach, and likewise in Hawaii. I want to make a real difference in my life. Now let's return to my father. He represents a mere drop in the ocean when compared to the Rockefellers of the world. However, now we represent *two* drops, because I am joining his cause. If I succeed in convincing 1000 or more people around the world to join us, we will begin to gain momentum and become more and more powerful. Ford is now also manufacturing electric cars for the masses, meaning this is no longer a product exclusively for the rich. Of course for now, you will have to pay a little bit more for the new technology. But remember, every time you drive past a gas station, you're making a return on your investment.

Let's do the math – that way, I can convince 5000 folks to join us instead of 1000. My father bought his car in Canada for $40,000 (although the price has dropped since last year). With all taxes in, the total cost of the car was $47,000. I can hear you say: that is a huge chunk of money for a car of that make and size. I agree, but let the math roll on. He received an $8000 credit back from the government as an environmental incentive. Our new total is $39,000.

Before his new electric acquisition, my father was driving a Nissan Murano. Filling his tank every week cost an average of $50. Over the course of a year, that's a saving of $2600. He plans to keep the electric car for 10 years because it came with an 8-year battery warranty. He told me he is confident the battery will remain reliable between years 8 and 10. For the sake of example, let's say the price of gas will remain the same (although it will probably increase). We are at a total of $26,000 in fuel savings over the total timeframe. Everyone knows that after 10 years, the resale value of any car is virtually $0, so let's say his car will have to go straight to the junkyard. Now let's do the same math as though my father had bought a new Nissan Murano instead of his Volt. The price is almost the same at $30,000 plus tax, a total of $35,000 (my father lives in Canada 6 months of the year and has always bought his cars there). Obviously in this scenario he would have to pay for gas: $50 per week, $2600 per year. Let's say he also plans to keep the vehicle for 10 years. In this scenario he will pay $26,000 in gas for the full 10-year period. The value of the vehicle at end of the term will be $0, just like the Volt. The final result is $26,000 saved in gas, but a $4000 higher sales price for the electric car versus the Murano. In the final analysis, which scenario makes you $22,000 richer (and the Rockefellers of the world $26,000 poorer)? My father is not only environmentally friendly, he is also wallet-friendly… towards himself. It's good business sense. You should do the same math when you want to buy a new vehicle. You will not only affect how the world evolves towards clean technologies, you will also be richer in the end. As momentum builds, we will all band together to take power back from the world's petroleum rulers. This small group of people has been in power for far too long. New, cleaner technologies have long been available, but the moneyed elite kills off innovation for the masses. I believe it is time for us all to correct this historical bump in the road with a new way of thinking collectively. Make no mistake, I love to succeed, but not by destroying the environment and certainly not by empowering trusts that manipulate politicians. You see, I believe in being environmentally conscious. We have to take care of Mother Nature, and the only home we have. I really do think that if you make money in that disrespectful manner, you will end up far poorer in the end. Including this chapter about doing the right thing is a choice. I fully endorse this choice because I believe good people always win in the end.

Your opportunity here is to change the world with us, for the better, one single little step at a time. The perfect song for this chapter is the old classic: Respect, by Aretha Franklin.

SUBMITTING YOUR BUSINESS PLAN

It's exciting to reach this chapter with you. I think we have a great opportunity to grow together. Our plane is still soaring at full speed in the right direction. All systems are Go for success. There are two pilots in the cockpit, so if one tires, the other can maintain our altitude.

I hope you have some great new business ideas in your portfolio, or at least in your head. If so, we want to hear from you. We would like to be part of your projects. Owning a business can be your one-way ticket to prosperity, as it was for me 14 years ago. Have you noticed that 98% of rich people own at least one business? Do you still think owning a business just isn't for you? You can still chase a corporate CEO position at Bank of America and become very wealthy. However, if you go that route, expect to pay at least half of that big salary back in taxes. If you prefer to own a business, then by all means, keep on reading. Let me first demolish the old saying people have repeated over and over again for a century: it takes money to make money. In this chapter, we offer you the exclusive opportunity to be funded by a top-flight organization. Keep in mind we do not work like a typical banking organization and do not make the same demands. We will not require you to pay a 50% cash down payment before funding your business. On the other hand, your project must be both impressive and realistic. We are looking for doers and entrepreneurs who want to build.

I know from experience that a lot of people have great ideas, but often, time and money are their biggest hurdles. Great business projects often fail at the start due to a shortage of funds. If you read my first book, you already know I was $75,000 short when trying to buy my first Tim Hortons franchise. At the time, the economy was in a lull and funding was scarce. Tremblay World has created a special division in which our group will analyze business plans from people looking for start-up funds for their business projects, providing them with a number of different options. The first option is a partnership mode, in which you retain a percentage ownership of the business and we hold a smaller percentage. The percentage will differ from project to project and must be negotiated first.

Keep in mind that our role is to provide funding, and yours is to create value and grow the business on the street level. In other words, we will not be involved in day-to-day business operations. You may, of course, benefit from the contacts we already have, but aside from that, the hard work must come from your side. The second option is to finance your project as with any other financial institution. The difference in this case is that your loan would be a private loan. Tremblay World is not the type of financial institution that is open to public. We are a private institution and our loan interest rates differ from one project to the next, depending on the risk involved and the type of business. The start-up phase of a business is always the hardest, and also when risk is greatest. You must be fully prepared before submitting your project. Nobody likes to waste his or her time. You will also have to demonstrate how and when your loan would be repaid, as with any other bank. If you fail at this part of the process, you will likely be advised to work out your project further before returning to resubmit it. Your first step is to build up your ideas, to analyze and know your market.

Finally, you must put everything down in writing in your business plan. You have to reach the point where all the puzzle-pieces fit together neatly in your head and you can therefore answer any questions we might ask. This, of course, is called the Big Picture.

As a standard practice, we only accept proposals made through the business program associated with The Billionaire Right Next Door. This program was designed to guide you through the entire step-by-step process of creating a proper business plan. We refer to it as a 12-day program, but anyone can do it more quickly by devoting the required time and energy. For more details on the program, please visit us at: www.billionairerightnextdoor.com This is the most complete program and perfectly fits our qualification requirements. We will not use business projects for any purposes other than funding or joint ventures. We will not use any ideas without the proper written authorization.

I sincerely hope we have the opportunity to fund your business project, and that we can work together. We have no minimum or maximum quota of businesses we intend to fund each year, but we do have project quality requirements. This is a great opportunity to fund new businesses, because I believe this is how wealth is created in a society. Show me a country where the percentage of businesses owned by individuals is low and I will show you a country that is probably poor.

We are looking to make a reasonable return on investment (ROI) and create entirely new projects. Most of all, we want you to succeed as a businessman (or woman), and are always searching for the perfect win-win scenario for all parties. The new businesses we now create no longer make significant demands on my time. Time is the precious currency of our lives, and is the subject of the next chapter. The perfect song for this chapter is: Taking Care of Business, by Bachman Turner Overdrive.

TIME

Tell me, dear reader: is time on your side, or against you? I don't ask the question idly, or to stress you out. Anyway, our flying altitude is such that our cellphones won't work anyway. We will not be disturbed until we land.

I ask simply because high achievers are also time masters. In his books, Donald Trump reminds us that he lives in the same tower that houses his office. He maximizes the time available in a day by taking just one elevator from home to to the office. That's an intelligent choice, and I'm pretty sure if you ask him why, he'd answer that time mastery gives him a competitive edge. When I see morning rush hour traffic, I see time wasted on a massive scale. Many people complain that they don't have any time. When you examine their daily routine, you quickly discover that they live at least one hour away from work. There are, of course, tons of good reasons behind that choice, but I still consider it a lousy one. If you are really serious about achieving your goals, you must seize control of your time the way Trump does and act differently from the masses. In business, if you want to run the show all by yourself, you will quickly discover that your time is consumed before you know it. You must single out a reliable employee and start thinking about delegating non-essential tasks. If you don't have any such employees, you are in trouble. You will have to invest time in hiring good employees and firing bad members of your team. And believe me, that is easier said than done. I've witnessed many managers who kept on bad staff simply because they were too lazy to take the time to start the hiring process over. That, my friends, is a recipe for disaster.

If you ask me how I invest my time, I have to be honest and admit that I am not at Trump's maximum level... but I am getting better every day. I would remind you that Trump and Tremblay both begin with the same two letters (Tr)... so perhaps we are not so different after all! In all seriousness, you will never see me mowing the lawn, much less cleaning windows. I am smart enough to book 5 appointments in the same time slot in my daily schedule, and I won't hesitate to start one off by saying: I've only got 10 minutes for you, so please speak quickly and get right to the point. That's how I work. I'm a fast talker and I expect the same from others. If you tell me you want to be rich, but you still mow your own lawn, I'll respond that there is a contradiction between your stated desire and what you really do.

Right now I am at a place in my life where, in the short to medium term, I need to consider hiring a full time cook at home. It's a weird situation, because I've never considered that before. It is strange to think about it; but on the logical side, how many hours of my time in a year are dedicated to preparing food and washing the dishes? I must admit: a lot − in fact, way too many. I would prefer to delegate that to a chef and spend time with my family when food is ready and on the table. This is quality time I don't want to mess with. The problem is that although I know I have to do it, I never have before, and so, inevitably, the decision took me out of my comfort zone. I can promise you that by the time I publish my next book, I will have a full-time cook at home. I've been pushed out of my comfort zone so often that it's *déjà vu* for me, and I will not let the situation defeat me. You will have to do the same in your life with your lawn-moving issue. If you already have: congratulations... but are you still shoveling the snow in your driveway?

Do as I have done, and draw up an inventory of stuff you can't or won't do in your life anymore. Let's imagine you can recapture this time and spend it working on your business plan, and that in return, that business will provide you with all the money you ever dreamt of in the future. Wouldn't mowing the lawn be a secondary task? You'd better believe it! In all seriousness, once you become successful, you will still have to conduct this exercise again and again if you want to propel yourself to the next level, and the next... Trump did the same thing many years ago when he bought his own private jet. At first you will find it strange to have this extra time on your hands. Think of your time usage as water in a glass. Typically, when you remove half the water from a glass, the empty space fills up again faster than you think. Therefore, you must carefully choose the new water you are going to add to your glass by constantly asking yourself: is this new addition going to help me achieve my medium- to long-term goals? Don't use up your new available time by cleaning your garage; instead, toss the task to your young nephew (the one who just wants to make a few bucks).

Use this new free time to start writing your next bestselling book. As you may recall, we have a very interesting and rewarding annual literary contest...When you are on vacation at the beach, why not read business how-to books instead of fiction or novels? Fiction is a great imaginative escape, but you will never use it in your daily reality. If you want to escape your daily life, you are probably investing your time in the wrong places. Have you ever wondered what your life would be like if you suddenly had the courage to make a 180-degree change? That is what my wife and I did in 2001: a complete turnaround, with no option to go back. I wonder what our lives would be like today if we hadn't made that turnaround in 2001. Nah... that's a bad thought. I prefer to stay focused and build our future. The perfect song for this chapter is: Time (Where did you go?), by Chantal Kreviazuk. If you have spare time in your life, then you are probably rich. I have time right now, and I'm using it to write this chapter on wonderful Waikiki beach, a natural setting that spurs creativity. The sound of waves is truly inspirational. Try it sometime and let me know how it works out for you. It works perfectly for me, because beaches are relaxing places where people are happy and have fun. Fun and happiness are contagious. The overall bonus is simply the opportunity to be on one of the amazing Hawaiian Islands. When I am here, I feel like the most privileged person in the world.

THE HIGH ACHIEVERS SOCIETY

While you are thinking about how to liberate more time in your life so you can eventually join me on Waikiki beach, I will tell you the story of the High Achievers Society and how it was created.

The High Achievers Society was created purely by chance. I was with my friend Micah last year, and we were talking about money and wondering why we have so much good fortune with it... Our conversation suddenly turned to discussing a new achievement competition. It would be a friendly competition geared toward reaching a certain level of net wealth, with the winner being the first to reach the goal. For the sake of confidentiality (Micah likes to keep his wealth on a low profile) I will not disclose the amount of our bet. We continued the conversation, saying: Wouldn't it be fun to create a club of people who aim for major achievements? A very private club, for golden boys... although not reserved exclusively for boys. More and more women are achieving great things in business as well. I told Micah it was a great idea – but what would be the membership criteria? He said members would have to own and operate a business with a minimum of 10 million dollars in annual sales. The High Achievers Society was born. The idea is simple: you get to hang around with successful people like us. There is no obligation to become a member of the club. You only have to qualify as a high achiever in your daily life. Members play golf together and also travel around the world. If the next club trip is to Bora Bora and that fits your schedule, you just notify us, and then pack for the flight. If you're too busy to join us, no matter: hopefully the next trip will work out. Mostly, these trips are dedicated to enjoying life, having fun, playing golf, snorkeling, relaxing at the beach and discussing things all the time. However, we also reserve time for we what we call High Achievers Society mastermind sessions. Usually, these trips would only include an exclusive group of 5 to 12 members. Each member explains his or her goals for the short, medium and long term to the rest of the group. We conduct reviews and follow-ups on what has occurred since the last trip.

Each member can take as much time as needed to explain all projects in detail. Other members may offer tips or suggestions at any time. Members need to be open to the views of others and ready to receive comments. We all want to see everyone in this club succeed. There are no specific rules; after all, we are friends, first and foremost. These mastermind sessions are magical; the level of energy created in the group is beyond any description. You have to experience it to truly understand. The High Achievers Society is not some club with a goal of reaching 600,000 members. That's just not going to happen. We want to maintain things at a family level. You will not find any specific club website, for now at least. Simplicity is the key. Whenever we want to organize events, we email our members for their thoughts. We then establish a final destination and dates in a subsequent email. The last step is to ask members to supply a deposit to confirm their spot. Club membership operates on an annual fee basis. Whenever we receive a new membership application, we consult everyone, and if all agree, the new member is officially welcomed into the club. Prospective new members must come with a referral from at least one existing member. Best of all, members can bring their loved ones and kids. Again, there are no set rules. Mastermind sessions are the only events that children cannot attend. In every other instance, members are free to do what they want, when they want. I describe the High Achievers Society here because we want you to join our group soon. I hope the info will ignite your inner drive to reach the next level and grow your business until it tops the magic number of 10 million dollars in annual sales. At that point, we will officially consider you a High Achiever world champion. It doesn't matter if it takes you 10 years to reach this level. We will still be here standing and waiting for you to join us.

I KNOW YOU

Throughout this book, we've been sitting and talking while our jet zooms towards success. I now feel that I know you. I hope you feel the same about me – if not, I've been doing a very bad job! I might have to use one of those parachutes myself.

In all seriousness, I would never give up that easily. Believe me when I say that I know you. You may wonder how that's possible when I've never met you in real life. My answer is: because deep down inside, we are all the same. We all want to be loved. We want to show to the world how great and special we are. We want to be recognized, and we want to be rich. We don't want to become rich to hurt people, but to change the world for the better. We also know that it's hard to change the world without the minimal amount of money. When we see our relatives, we expect them to recognize and remember who we are. When we achieve a milestone, we want to be acknowledged. We want to grow and experience different things. We love our kids. We love life. We love the god we believe in (no matter what name you use). We love to travel and see the world. We love to have fun. We love to meet friends for dinner. We love to eat great food. The list goes on and on, right? See, I wasn't too far from the truth. We all have a different outside appearance and ego, but what we really want at the elemental level is basically the same. We are somewhat built on the same frame. I like to observe people all the time, because I am curious by nature. I always ask myself: what drives this person? And you can observe a person's level of drive fairly easily just by watching how fast he walks and moves. Just try this exercise once. Imagine yourself as an actor in Hollywood. Your challenge consists in playing the role of a billionaire. If no specific figure comes to your mind, choose a person like Richard Branson.

Fix this image in your mind and ask yourself how Richard would act in his daily life. I am sure you see Richard as a confident man who thinks and believes he can achieve anything in life. He probably walks confidently, don't you think? Now you get the picture. Walk as he would as you make your daily rounds to the drugstore, dry cleaner's, bank and grocery store. Internalize your Richard Branson for the whole day and act exactly as he would. If everyone in your town knows you, then spend the day in a different one; even more so if you are naturally shy and think the experience will be intimidating. Dress the way you think Branson would and go for it. Walk and act like him. Take note of how people look at you, open the door for you and smile at you. Pay attention to the kind of respect you receive. People will perceive you exactly as you perceive yourself. You have to live out this concept to understand it. Reading is not enough; you have to experience this in the flesh.

At the end of the day, take out a sheet of paper and explain what the experience was like in as much detail as possible. Did you enjoy the experience? Did it feel artificial? Did you feel you were in the right place? It is important to play this role out because, after all, this is what you will be in the future – successful. Once you become successful, you can't go back and act like the world's poorest person. So practice this role more often. If you fall in love with your role, why not adopt it on a daily basis? As a youngster in school, I was a combination of the shy student and the class clown. I always attracted the attention of the troublemakers. In a way, I was the spark. Almost every person who is famous now was shy back in school. But somewhere, somehow, they decided it was time to evolve and change the role they were playing.

Act today like the person you want to be and you will turbocharge the time required to get there. Don't wait for the perfect time. The only perfect time is now. Don't worry; you are not the only person who needs to practice this exercise. I do, as well. I have to act and work on my new role every day. The good news is that every day, I get better at it, and you will too. My trick is to fix an image of the finished product of myself in my head at all times. If you find it exhausting to fix that image in your head, you're probably just not used to doing it. It's like playing golf: hit the course and just try and then retry. Nobody is any good at golf at first. My guess is that even Tiger Woods wasn't very good when he hit his first ball. Practice was his best friend. I am a huge fan of golf because it a hard game to master. As you already know, I approach things that are hard to master as a challenge. I find that the best way to recognize a person's true desire to succeed is to hit the golf course together. People reveal themselves on the course – both their good and bad attributes. Have you ever played a round of golf with a partner who wanted to quit the game because he wasn't hitting the ball right that day? If so, I strongly suggest you never get involved in any kind of business with that person. Business is also a hard game to master, so being with the right partner is crucial.

CHANGING PLACES

Let's pretend that you and I suddenly switched places. You would take my life and I would take yours, like that old movie where two newborn babies are mistakenly given to the wrong mother.

What would you do with my life? You really only have two options: would you continue my actual work and keep building my financial empire, or would you party and run wild? If you chose the second option, that means my wealth curve would suddenly break and start turning downward, eventually crashing to the ground. Believe me, it's easy to screw up big, even if you have millions of dollars on your hands. For my part, I would take a day off from your job or business by calling in sick. I might not necessarily be sick, but I would definitely need the time to analyze exactly where I was. I would need to know if my new life was in North Dakota, California, Arizona or elsewhere. North Dakota? Okay, then I would need to know if I work for a paycheck or run my own business. Am I married or divorced? One kid, several or none? Don't worry, your family wouldn't be involved in this. We can pretend they don't know we have switched places. It's a secret between you and me.

Next, I would want a clearer picture of my financial state. I would immediately head to the computer and start a new Excel spreadsheet. I would begin the list with my new asset situation (house value, cars, money in the bank, accumulated pension funds, investments, property...). After the list of assets, I would draw up the list of my new debts and creditors (credit card balances, mortgage, student loans...). The total amount of assets minus debts would reveal my new net worth situation. If I had a total net worth of a million dollars or more, I would still be a millionaire and the rest of the game would be fairly easy. If I were below the million-dollar mark, I would have to work on my balance sheet immediately. I would take a closer look at my debt – where does it hurt the most? Do I carry balances with 18% interest or higher? If so, I would shred those credit cards right away. My job for the next several weeks would be to combine all my unpaid bad debt balances in one place, with a rate lower than 18%. This is called a debt consolidation loan. If I could get a 9% rate for this new loan, I would have my first win in my new situation.

Next I would pay off this single new loan at a faster rate whenever I could. I would set goals. I would keep my existing car for at least the next 10 years. I would cut down on unnecessary expenses like the big cable TV package (I hardly need the 200 channel package, since I don't even watch TV). If the house were a castle without the salary to justify it, I would sell it for a smaller one (with a smaller mortgage). I always consider it a bad idea to look rich if the bank account is empty. I would squeeze unnecessary expenses to a point where I could call the bank and ask them to automatically set aside 10% of my weekly paycheck in savings. That is my minimum savings requirement. That's how I have been saving for the past 20 years or so, and I will always maintain that sound financial habit, even when I hit the one billion dollar mark. My wife and I have saved at a 25% rate for at least the past 10 years. We're not cheap; we just have all the possessions we need, and then some.

Going back to my new life in North Dakota, I would aim to become a millionaire within 5 years. I would write down this goal and timeframe on a big board and display it somewhere in the house where I could see it frequently every day. I would call the Tim Hortons U.S. head office in Columbus, Ohio and ask them to send me the franchise application ASAP – even if I did not currently qualify on the financial side. I know from experience that when Tim Hortons really likes your profile, they can sometimes move mountains to get you on board. I would try to find the missing funds from inside my new circle of family members and friends by selling them on how great Tim Hortons is and why I need their help to qualify. I would tell them how and when they could expect to get their money back. I would also tell them how much interest they would earn from this loan deal. Then I would send my application to the Tim Hortons head office. I would call the franchise department every week until they got tired of me and granted me an interview. In the interview I would inform them that while funds might currently be tight for the down payment, I would find the missing money one way or another. I would also inform them about a great high-traffic location I'd spotted in North Dakota. I would be so enthusiastic in the interview that they would have no choice but to choose me (again, but they wouldn't know the whole story about our life change).

A couple of months later, in my new store, I would again work like crazy, 7 days a week. I would be involved in my community so that everybody knew the store. Remember, when you do a great job at Tims, success always shows up. Next, I would grow from one store to two or maybe even three. In less than five years, I would be millionaire again. And if not with Tims, I would definitely be involved in another business and still end up a millionaire. The perfect song for this chapter is: I Lived, by One Republic. Living above your means can kill anyone financially. If you don't think this chapter is realistic, I have a real-life story that I hope will erase all your doubt. The story is about two brothers: Mohammad and Abdul. In 2000, they emigrated from Afghanistan to Canada with only $200 in their pockets. At first, they worked hard to pay the rent and save the rest. Mohammad worked as a baker at the Tim Hortons nearest to where I lived. I was a new Tims franchisee and sometimes had to borrow products I needed from Mohammad's franchisee. What I didn't know was that Mohammad dreamt of buying his own Tims franchise one day. He finally made his official application three years later. At first, our franchisor wasn't willing to give the brothers the opportunity to prove themselves. In response, they did the only thing they could: they called again and again to follow up on their application, almost to the level of harassment. I guess the head office grew sick and tired of the phone calls, and finally said: OK guys, we'll give you the chance to prove what you can do. They finally had their first store, but it was in the absolute worst location you could imagine. Their low sales volume made it virtually impossible to avoid big losses. This challenge didn't stop the two brothers. They arrived at the store on that first day with the firm intention of turning lemons into lemonade.

To ensure they would not fail, they worked night and day, rotating their shifts 7 days a week nonstop for the whole first year. In the first month, the competitor across the street closed down. That, combined with the great job they were doing, meant sales volume doubled after the first weeks and doubled again before the end of their first year of operation. The store was transformed from a lemon into a moneymaking machine virtually overnight. The head office was so impressed by the results that they had to sell them another store. Ten years after the two brothers arrived in Canada with $200, they owned and operated 10 stores together and had both become multimillionaires. They are still successful today, but now they have so much money they just don't know what to do with it! It's a good problem to have. These two brothers are hard workers, but also very smart businessmen. I like these guys; whenever we meet, we talk for hours. They are living proof that anything is possible when you really want it badly enough.

IT'S THE THOUGHT THAT COUNTS

Reader, this chapter is a very important one. You must be open to it. If you do not act in accordance with this Law, it will be difficult to achieve your goals. I want to be honest with you, because this is the truth. You will receive abundance in life only if you give first without expecting anything in return.

Let me share a personal real-life story with you to help make the point. Your opportunity here is to change the way you act and think about giving in your day-to-day life. We can simply call this the Law of Compensation or Return, where everything you give must return to you one way or another, on a greater level. I hope you will take this subject seriously. It was last year, on my birthday, and I was on the golf course. It was a beautiful sunny day. I always like to take a day off of each year on my birthday and do nothing else but golf. My round was going very well and I was matched with three other guys I hadn't met before. I don't know why, but every time I'm matched with folks I don't know, they always end up being fun and interesting people.

I was half way through the 9th hole, eating my sandwich, when my cellphone rang. It was my real estate manager in Michigan, who takes care of my tenants and my properties there. He never calls me unless something major has broken or needs to be replaced. Generally, when he calls, I know it's going to cost me money. I said to myself before answering: the fridge is probably broken; I hope it's not the roof! Then I instantly recalled that, in this case, I'd replaced the roof when I bought the house for $27,000 from the bank (a foreclosure). Believe me, at that low-ball price, I didn't mind replacing the roof. When I answered, Jake told me he was calling concerning our tenant. We were at the lease renewal anniversary, and a rent increase had already been agreed to the year before and was taking effect automatically. Jake told me our tenant Jeanice was not in a position to afford the rent increase. Her husband had just lost his job and they were living on one salary. They would probably need to move out of the house if the rent increase took place. My choice was easy.

I told Jake to let her know the rent would remain unchanged, and asked him to keep the tenants happy. If you have investment properties, you know this is a wise business decision. Whenever a tenant moves, money is always required to restore the house back to rent-ready condition. Moreover, up to three months of rent may be lost while you look for a new qualified tenant. Finally, there is always the risk that you will end up with a bad new tenant, even if your manager conducts the requisite research, credit and criminal background checks. All of that can cost thousands of dollars. I knew I'd made the right decision.

After the call, I returned to my game, and the thought occurred: let's test the Law of Return to the max here. The Law of Return teaches us that when we give, we receive back from life. The fact that I was leaving the lease unchanged was a double gift for Jeanice. First, it was obviously financial relief, and second, she could forget the stress of having to pack up, move out and find a new place. But that wasn't enough for me. I decided to send her a handwritten letter to let her know I understood the hard time she was going through, and to tell her to keep faith. Then, a small inner voice of kindness said: along with your letter, why not send her a $100 gift card from Tim Hortons? The chain has stores in Michigan. It was a pretty good idea, so I promised the inner voice that I would think about it. In fact, this was a very innovative way to test the Law. Then I wrapped up my golf game and almost forget the whole thing. No matter what I did next, I was already feeling good about having told Jake to leave the lease unchanged.

The following day, that little voice came back to remind me of the bargain we'd struck on the golf course. I immediately looked for a sheet of paper and a pen, and started to write my letter to Jeanice. I reminded her of yesterday's decision to leave the lease unchanged. I also mentioned that I knew her husband had just lost his job, and that I understood hard times. I continued by asking her to keep faith, as I was convinced a new and better job was on its way. I finished by asking her to accept a $100 Tim Hortons gift card. A Steak and Cheese Panini sandwich and a great cup of coffee are always a winner for the soul. I signed the letter and told my inner voice: mission accomplished. My inner voice reminded me that the gift card was not inside the letter, and I reminded the voice that it was Sunday, and I would finish the whole process on Monday. Everyone was happy. Monday came, and naturally, the voice was there. Don't worry, I said, I will do it today. Suddenly, I had a flash realization: I'm at my house in Canada, and Jeanice lives in the U.S. Different country, different currency! It would be stupid to send a $100 gift card Jeanice couldn't use... and so the inner voice said: Plan B required.

Luckily, my house in Canada is located less than an hour from the U.S. border. I decided to jump in my car and head to the Tim Hortons in Messina, NY. When I told the U.S. border patrol agent my story, he was stunned. I admitted it was kind of weird, but told him I had to do this. In a stroke of luck, he let me enter the U.S. without any further questions. Also luckily, the Tim Hortons store was 5 minutes from the border, near the Casino. After eating my Crispy Chicken lunch combo, I returned to the cashier and asked to buy the $100 gift card. For some strange reason, my U.S. credit card was not working. She told me the only other option available was the nearest ATM. I was starting to feel like I would never reach the finish line, but a quick visit to the ATM and back and I finally had the gift card. Believe it or not, it cost me $3 to get the $100 cash! Convenience store ATMs tend to be pricey.

Back at the Canadian border, I had to explain my strange story once again. The border agent commented that it had been a short visit, and looked at me like I had committed a crime. When she finally saw my transaction receipt, she said: that's a nice gesture, you can go ahead, have a good day. Oh yeah, I forget to mention, the Cornwall and Messina border crossings have bridge fees: $3 to go to the U.S., and $3 to get back! What an adventure... but still, it was for a good and personally fulfilling cause. When you believe in something, there is no cost. And I believed in this. I hope Jeanice will read this book one day, just to see how much of a challenge it was for me to get that special Tim Hortons U.S. gift card. When I finally got home, I was looking forward to closing the loop of the experience. I reminded myself that the Law of Return states that you have to give and feel great about the process. It also teaches us to do so without expecting or wanting something in return. I was expecting to receive nothing more from the experience than the good feeling that I had made a small difference in the life of my tenant. When I reached the mailbox at the corner of my street and put the letter inside, I was simply thinking: this is for you Jeanice, and all the best. And so I turned to my inner voice and said: I told you I would see this through to the end. I heard nothing back, so I concluded the voice was very happy and proud of me. I don't understand why the inner voice is so present when it's time to achieve something, and disappears so quickly when everything is perfectly done. It would be nice to hear the voice say: good job, Dan, I'm proud of you. I guess that job is exclusively up to us! No kidding – I offer congratulations to myself, because 99.9999% of the time nobody else will. I'm going to assume the same is true for you.

Now, you'll never guess what happened next. I wasn't expecting this at all, but a week and a half after my generosity towards Jeanice, I received a letter from the government. The Internal Revenue Service informed me they had made a mistake in their calculations for the previous year, and I would soon receive a check for $8030.59! Can you believe that? I am accustomed to paying large amounts of money to the government because I make profits everywhere I turn. It's only normal to pay taxes when you make money. I'm certainly not used to receiving money from them. Five days after receiving the letter, a check arrived in the exact amount of $8030.59. That's a large return in such a small period of time, don't you think? I photocopied the check as proof in case anyone didn't believe me. I like to think the check was sent to me by the supreme intelligence (you can call it Gd if you want) because of what I had done two weeks earlier. I believe great things happen in life when you are kind and generous towards others. The perfect song for this chapter is: Angel, by Sarah McLachlan. Angels are part of my life; I've known that for many years. Do you have examples of your own acts of kindness or generosity towards friends, family members, loved ones or strangers that have brought you unexpected returns (money, help, love) as mine did? My goal is to be kind again; the experience was a clear success. I never received any news from Jeanice afterwards, but I assume she was happy to receive that unexpected letter.

Next time you are in the drive-thru lane at a quick service restaurant, pay for the order of the car behind you, with no other intention than just doing something good in your day. Just remain secure in the knowledge that something great will happen to you, because the Law works every time. Have you ever noticed that the richest people in the world are also the largest philanthropists? Certainly, they can choose to give or not – so why are they so generous? It's certainly not just for the tax savings; there are plenty of loopholes available if they want to work that out. My guess is that they have perfectly mastered the Law of Return. Not to be outdone, my wife and I donate more than 10 percent of our income to charity organizations every year. Our favourite one is the Tim Hortons Children's Foundation. Since its inception in 1975, this fabulous non-profit organization has sent 120,000 children from low-income families to one of their 6 summer camps across North America. I absolutely love what they do and I'm proud to donate and support them financially every year. I call this principle: giving without expectation. The more I give, the more I receive.

Most people find this principle too simplistic and too good to be true. All I can say in response is that those who laugh are the same people who are a thousand miles from their goals. Period. Don't be foolish. If you wait to receive before giving, you will wait for a long, long time. To me, that would be like waiting for water before turning the faucet on, or waiting for light before flipping on the switch. The fact is that billions of people on Earth act in direct opposition to this Law. Please don't be one of them. Waiting to get what you want before offering the slightest effort on your part is a bad recipe destined for very bad results. Life just does not work that way. That is why so many people get so little out of life – not because they don't want great things in life, but because they are unwilling to give first and receive more later. I would like to thank you for accompanying me through this chapter. I want you to follow my path to success. That path has a specific set of rules that must be followed. Your job is to take them seriously and apply them on a daily basis. You will sometimes need to be as innovative as I was in my strange little project, but I urge you to try even if people look at you as though you are weird. I certainly seemed weird to the border guards – on both sides – but that didn't stop me. In fact, other people's judgments are unimportant.

Other people's judgments are there only to test you, to see if you will follow through. Stick to your beliefs and act in the best interests of all – not just for your own benefit, but for the greater good.

AN ECONOMICS UPDATE

We are entering the waking part of our trip, and I want to inform you about the kind of world we live in. This chapter concerns the state of the economy. Frankly, it's almost never in great shape, so there's no point in waiting for the perfect moment. Money can be made during the worst and best periods alike. I rarely take cues from the economy before I make my moves, because as I said, there is no perfect moment. The perfect moment is always now. Your priorities are the product you want to promote, and your target market. A good product is a good product, and people will buy it no matter what kind of shape of the economy is in.

Please approach this chapter as an offer of crucial information. You will end up better informed afterwards, even if the negative events listed below never materialize. Human beings are adaptive; we can conceive of solutions or new regulations to improve efficiency and also control greed. I am an optimist. To me, the greater the amount of people who are aware of the systemic risks, the greater the chance we can manage them and learn. Economics is one of my favorite subjects. When you know the history of economic cycles, you can predict the ones to come. I understand that not everybody enjoys this subject, but if you are serious about accumulating wealth, you must become an expert in how economic cycles work. Forget about the financial pseudo-specialists on TV, they are nothing more than mutual funds salesmen. They can explain why an event has occurred in the past but are very bad at predicting the future.

Negative events in the past have all been created by central driving forces: greed, speculation and the abuse of credit. When you buy any investment product and your main goal is to make a quick resale profit rather than use it for yourself, you are a speculator. If you are speculating on your own, you do not pose a large problem for the financial system as a whole. Problems arise when millions of individuals are simultaneously sold on the idea that they will make money on one particular popular product. My favorite instance was the Tulip Mania of 1636. Let's face it – if they could successfully sell the masses on the bizarre idea that three tulip bulbs had the same value as a house, they can convince the masses of anything, at any time. Who are "they"? They are the small group of wealthy plutocrats who most benefit from any economic bubble. They are the people who start and spark the propaganda machine. They are the ones who want economic bubbles to last, and who promulgate them by attempting to convince the masses that the event is not, in fact, a bubble. Should the bubble burst, they have very little to lose.

Always consider who has the most to win in any cycle, and who risks losing the most. In every bubble, there are two counterparts, or two players if you prefer. In the case of the 2008 real estate bubble in the U.S., the two players were: house buyers and speculators, and Wall Street (the banks). Who had the most at risk? My perspective is clear: house buyers, because when they signed the purchase papers, they were risking their credit and all the assets they had previously accumulated. The bankers were the clear winners. Every time a mortgage was signed, they immediately pocketed big, fat commissions; but the beauty is that they could also double back and avoid all mortgage default risk by reselling the mortgages in bundles to pension funds and other employee institutions. Thanks to that little magic trick, the mortgages were removed from their books. Imagine you are the bank. You incur no risk because you can instantly resell it. Therefore, what would your daily business goal be? I'd guess the bank's goal would be to sign off on tons of new mortgages, no matter who was applying. You can surely see greed rearing its ugly head here. Imagine for a moment that you work at one of the Big Three car manufacturers and, in 2007, you bought a bigger house, twice the size of your previous one (with double the mortgage). You believed that real estate would only increase in value. You signed the papers and took on all the risks, both good and bad. Next thing you know, it's 2008, and your 600K home is plummeting in value, bottoming out at 250K in less than a year. You now have a negative equity loan, meaning the balance you have to pay off is greater than the residual value of your house. Worse, your employer just announced that because the company pension fund bought a large amount of toxic mortgage-backed assets from banks (perhaps even including your loan), the pension fund has lost 20% of its value. They have no choice but to ask for higher pension contributions from all employees.

But wait – the story isn't over. Nobody is buying new cars because the economy is in such a bad shape. Your employer announces they will have to cut all the company's night shifts, along with their 400 employees. You are on a bad luck streak, because that's your shift. It's a real nightmare, isn't it? As a result, you stopped paying your mortgage, defaulted and lost all your bank credit. Your mortgage became worthless, thanks to your pension fund. This story may be not yours, but it was the story of millions of Americans. Now let's look at what happened on the bank's side. The bank pocketed its commission in 2007 when you bought your house, and resold your mortgage to your pension fund. The bank no longer had anything to do with your mortgage when you began to default on it. Banks that kept too many bad mortgages on their books in 2008 ran into deep trouble, but of course, they could count on bailout funds from the taxpayers. That must be a joke, right? I mean, they created this whole global mess in the first place (because your pension fund wasn't the only fund that bought these toxic assets) and now we've bailed them out. At least the financial institutions were hit with record fines many years later for creating this financial engineering disaster. Still, I don't think anyone went to jail. Too much greed is bad for the system. And so I ask you again: which player was the real winner in this bubble – regular citizens and taxpayers, or Wall Street (the banks)? If you are not on the winning side, I suggest you to do your best not to be among the losers. Nobody was obliged to jump into this frenzy. Admittedly, they (Wall Street) did a very good job selling the idea of real estate as a guaranteed pathway to wealth. Don't get me wrong: buying real estate *is* a very good way to become a millionaire, but not in the midst of a frenzy. In 1700, Tulip Mania created a financial frenzy, but whether it's tulip bulbs or real estate, there is no difference in the outcome whenever people lose all logical perspective. When that happens, a financial tsunami is right around the corner. The only thing we don't know is precisely when it will hit. History constantly repeats itself. Today, the mortgage crisis is behind us and normal levels of activity seem to be returning. However, if you want to foresee the source of the next crisis, I suggest you watch where Wall Street is heading and observe their activity from the outside. I must admit, they still have to work hard to pay off the huge penalties levied on them by the U.S. government. I approve of that scenario, because at least some type of justice has been served. I will never take Wall Street's side because of the damage they can cause. Greed will always re-emerge as a force on Wall Street.

If you take an "outside the box" perspective on Wall Street and look beyond the fact that they are still paying huge financial penalties, you will discover they are also once again making very good money. Given how low interest rates are, Wall Street is currently pushing high yield junk-rated stocks. They are very effective in selling these products to people foolish enough to listen. Their strategy is simply to convince people they are missing the boat if they fail to invest in this popular product category. I'm guessing that Wall Street sells these products to their more foolish clientele with one hand, while betting with the other that their junk products will default. That's exactly what they did with the Greek government. Financial institutions loaned the government huge amounts of money, knowing it could never repay – then turned around and bet against Greek government bonds. Unsurprisingly, they did so very successfully and made tons of money, but you know the rest of the story. After the deal, the Greek people suffered terribly. The economic situation is only slightly improved today, with unemployment still at 25%. I'm not saying the Greeks aren't also responsible for their past mismanagement and poor decisions… but why keep kicking someone when he's already down? One hand offers him a loan, the other sticks a knife in his back. Wall Street is like a shiver of sharks, and they like bloody scenarios. You do not want to be the small fish in the middle. If junk bonds and junk stocks are such a good investment, why doesn't Wall Street buy them all? After all, they have almost all the money in the world.

It would only take a small interest rate hike to push those high yield stock companies into default. Banking a 7% interest return on your investment is great, but the goal is also to get your initial capital investment back. Look closely at the debt level ratio. Investing in high yield stock companies with a debt level ratio of more than 100% is like playing with fire. You're certain to get burned one day. Credit default swaps represent another very lucrative market for Wall Street. Credit default swaps are an insurance policy that large pension funds like to take out to protect themselves in case of a default on their investments. Let's pretend I have a large pension fund and I am looking for a return better than 1%. That will require taking some risks. The problem is, pension funds cannot invest directly in high yield corporate junk stocks because the funds are regulated by the government and that type of investment is judged to be too risky. That makes perfect sense for everyone, since pension funds are employee contributions and the money must be invested wisely and safely. That's when a credit default swap company like AIG swoops in. AIG tells the pension fund they will insure the default risk, in return for a relatively small premium. Since AIG is rated AA by Moody's, the pension fund can take much bigger investments risks based on the fact that the risk of default is now insured and covered. As when you buy home insurance, the amount you pay each year for your coverage premium is minimal compared with your coverage amount. But these days, instead of using credit default swaps to insure their investments, people are using them to speculate on assets they don't own. That's like gambling in a casino. How would you feel if I bought insurance on your house and bet that it would burn down? You would probably find the idea strange at the very least, and more likely think it should be prohibited, because it would mean I was hoping to see your house burn down.

Moreover, you might even be afraid that I would plan for that very eventuality, and pay someone to make it happen. You are right – and thank goodness people can't take out fire insurance on buildings they don't own. Why should the situation be any different for this type of financial product? Credit default swaps were originally marketed to help hedge investment risk. Now, this market is just a huge casino where hedge funds and private banks gamble on a massive scale instead of investing the money in the real economy – or Main Street, if you prefer. The problem is that the credit default swap market has vastly increased in popularity and proportion over the years. Today, the swap market represents an astounding 36 trillion dollars worldwide. To give you an idea of how huge that number is, the world GDP (the real economy) is 75 trillion dollars per year. Regular insurance companies providing home insurance are regulated by rules and laws. The reason is simple: government regulators want to make sure insurance companies will be financially solid enough to cover losses in the event of a major natural disaster. That is the important difference between a regular insurance company and a credit default swap insurance company. The latter is not regulated the way the former is. Liquidity ratios are not regulated at AIG. As we witnessed during the last major financial crisis involving Lehman Brothers, everyone is financially interconnected worldwide. If the default is isolated, it's not a big deal. The pension fund or contract beneficiary will most likely get their money back. But what if a major disruptive financial event occurs again in the near future? In that case, everyone will want to exercise their credit swap contracts at the same time. We all know there is absolutely no way AIG will have enough money to cover and honor all those contracts at once. The reason is simple: the overall liquidity ratios AIG carries are ridiculously low compared to the amounts they would have to cover in the case of a negative financial event. Remember, there is very little regulation. History shows us that when there are few regulations in place, greed takes control and contributes to the next crisis. In the instance of a major negative financial event, buying credit swap contracts would be as worthwhile as buying air. During boom years, companies like AIG engaged in selling credit default swap contracts are laughing all the way to the bank, because profits are through the roof. They also know that if a major event should occur, the government and the taxpayers will be called upon to clean up the mess.

If you think people today are more aware than ever, think again. Nobody ever mentions these systemic risks. Have you heard anything in the news today addressing the subject of this chapter? Certainly not, since the TV pundits only discuss events that have already occurred. Our job is to be aware that these things could happen any day. I sincerely hope that the regulators wake up and prevent these guys from constantly speculating, and force them to do what they should be doing: loaning money to fuel the real economy. Have you ever noticed how gamblers behave in a casino? Daytime and nighttime cease to matter as they spend every hour at the tables, doing nothing but moving around chips and turning over cards. They don't contribute much to the real economy. Sometimes, they grab a sandwich and a soda just to stay alive, making a rare contribution to the real economy, but the rest of the time they might as well be ghosts. I don't think today's global financiers are much different. They move tons of money around on a daily basis, but that money does nothing substantive beyond changing places. Why have I brought this up? Our job is not only to become immensely wealthy, but also to stay wealthy for life, no matter what bad scenario may arise. It is critically important for you to understand how the economy works, and the important role it plays in your life. These guys are like financial atomic and nuclear bombs, always at risk to go off, and we must be aware and prepare just in case. What would happen if one of those bombs exploded? We've already seen what can happen with the AIG situation of 2008. The exact same scenario can re-occur today.

AIG sold default insurance on toxic real estate assets to almost every pension fund in the world. When people recognized the toxicity of these supposedly insured products, they also recognized that AIG was far from the solid and liquid company everyone thought it was. Only government institutions had the wherewithal to bail out the mess. I simply cannot understand why AIG is allowed to conduct the very same business today, even though the company does not have much more liquidity than it did then. On the positive side of the ledger, the U.S. government made money on the bailout after the recovery. Of course, the next crisis won't be erupting in the U.S. real estate market. I would instead foresee a default by a country that carries too much debt. AIG sells credit default swaps on almost all government bonds. If a country were to default on its debt, then tons of contracts would fall due, as we saw in 2008. AIG would not have enough liquidity to support the claims and... here we go again, sunk into a new crisis. The problem is that credit default swaps present the false impression that the risk is fully covered. With the impression as their faulty guide, people tend to choose a higher investment risk level than they normally would.

I would remind you that the world's debt level to GDP is more than 300%, if we consider nation-state and corporate debts all together. That figure is quite high, but surely not unsustainable. I think we should all be wary when it comes to debt. How do you manage yours? It's hard to exert any control over our government spending, but you have full control over your own debt level. Nobody forces you to sign the papers. And so, I advise you to use debt carefully. Your government has printing presses in case it runs into financial trouble. We don't have that option available on our side.

Why are our governments so heavily in debt? You will find a large part of the answer on the revenue side. Corporations, like everybody's favorite Internet powerhouse whose name starts with 'G', are now global corporate superpowers. They are so powerful I would consider them to be the new Rockefellers of our era – although Rockefeller was concentrated mainly in the U.S, while these corporations sell their virtual products everywhere. Since these corporations are active in every country, they can decide where to be taxed on their corporate profits. If you were them, you would probably choose the country with the lowest corporate tax rate... and that is what they do. This is known as financial engineering, and for now, it remains legal. Let's pretend that a big tech corporation takes billions in sales out of the American economy in exchange for virtual products (which might as well be air). That's a great deal for the tech corporation, whose profits are through the roof, as you can well imagine. Let's further imagine that this corporation makes 25 billion dollars in sales in the U.S. From that figure, 19 billion dollars is profit. The tech corporation is incorporated in the Bahamas and pays almost $0 back to the U.S. government in corporate tax. Repeat this process over and over with 100 tech corporations, and you get the picture. Big tech corporations grab with one hand and toss back peanuts with the other. Worse, their huge profits remain on that island, generating absolutely nothing. Sure, these tech companies re-invest a small portion of their untaxed profits in research and development, but don't be fooled: the lion's share stays on the island and contributes nothing to the real economy. Now let's return to our government, which has gotten screwed big time by these corporations. The government must pay for Medicaid, staff, highways, schools, hospitals, the military... you name it. These corporations are literally laughing at us. But the situation isn't funny anymore. Our governments have no choice but to create large deficits to fund the missing money. Incidentally, that deficit belongs to you, and will belong to your children and grandchildren. I often wonder if and when someone will stand up and say: enough is enough, we need to pay our policemen and firemen, and that money has to come from *somewhere*.

I dislike corporations that don't play fair, laughing at their customers and their own home country – I really don't. Trust me when I tell you that I never buy or use any of their virtual products. That is my protest vote. I know that's the only way to compel them to change their bad habits, by hitting them where it hurts the most: on the sales side, in the wallet. I admire companies like Coca-Cola – not for their sugar-loaded products, but for their recognition that the company's real value lies not in its bottling plants, but in its name and reputation. I firmly believe than when you damage your image and reputation, you will have to pay a huge price one day. Just look at the tobacco companies: in the 1970s, everyone thought they where untouchable. Since then, we've watched them crumble under countless lawsuits paying the plaintiffs record financial damages – and the story is far from over. When you know perfectly well that your actions are devastating, and do so deliberately anyway for profit, your days are numbered.

Believe it or not, some Americans think the deficit doesn't matter because we will never repay it. They forcefully argue that the U.S. is the world's only superpower, and can therefore do whatever it wants and spend however it wants without limit, because nobody can do anything about it. I believe that's a very dangerous way of thinking. I remember my history classes from school. Over the centuries, empires have risen and fallen, like the Roman Empire – the Superpower of its time, which collapsed after 700 years in power. Nobody at the time could have predicted that calamity... nevertheless, it is part of history. Many great societies failed before the Romans. Long after the Romans, England was a superpower that literally ruled the world during the beginning of the manufacturing revolution. They also failed to keep their empire intact. Overconfidence kills. Take those examples to heart and remember that previous success will never make you immune to failure.

There was a time when I thought that everything I touched would turn to gold. It worked for a while, but eventually the tides turned, and I was smart enough to recognize my mistakes before it was too late, correct them, and acknowledge that I was not immune to bad luck. I've written this chapter to show you that in business, the sky isn't always clear blue. We must adapt, as we must in life in general. In a financial nightmare scenario, I would suggest that you keep liquid assets on hand. The reason is simple: it is hard to sell property and illiquid assets when the economy is shaky. You don't want to end up in a position where you can't pay your day-to-day bills. It's also not a bad idea to have a small quantity of physical silver or gold. I call this my End of the Financial World Insurance Policy. If the financial system ever collapses completely, you will be in a great position if you own gold or silver coins. This is not alarmist, just advice to plan for the best and worst possible scenarios, just in case. I am not an activist. Quite simply, I was raised and taught to be fair and do good things for the greater good of all. Those are very simple principles we all remember from childhood. Why should they change when we grow up? We knew what the right thing to do was. We still remember. I would like to end the chapter by stating that I am far from an activist – I am an optimist, and I believe we will all succeed by changing what doesn't work and makes no sense financially. We have the power to do this collectively, especially with the advent of online social networks.

The perfect song for this chapter is: You Get What You Give, by New Radicals. Let's move forward to the next chapter. I hope you found this one interesting to read and learned something new.

JAPAN, TWO YEARS LATER

Keeping up with current trends gives you an edge for the future, which is why I include chapters on economics in my books. Most economists don't provide information properly, for a very simple reason: they have products to sell you, like mutual funds. I don't have any products like that for sale, so I can offer you some simple and effective explanations that will deepen your understanding.

In my first book I predicted trouble ahead, coming from the faraway island of Japan, the famed Land of the Rising Sun (and economic clouds). My prediction has yet to materialize, and I am glad. Like anyone else, I don't like crises and unstable financial environments. I'm offering this follow-up because there have been new developments in the past two years, and I would like to comment and share my point of view. My overall prediction has not changed. This country is bankrupt and there is no way anyone can change or fix core problems in the short term. My prediction was logical, and based on the fact that more people die in Japan every day than are born. I've yet to see a walking dead body spending money in a shopping center. The same holds true for new home purchases. By definition, dead people don't buy stuff and don't contribute to the economy anymore. Worse, the country has kept its borders closed to immigrants since time immemorial. Apparently, they don't like new foreign citizens, and having babies has become too expensive for them. I'm not sure if this story is true, but I've even heard that the new wave of teenagers don't like making love and prefer staying home alone. Wow! Those are not the ingredients for a brighter, vibrant future or for economic vitality. Right now, the population of Japan is 127 million; in 2050 it is projected to be 84 million. Can you imagine a country loosing a third of its population in such a short time? It seems perfectly easy to understand… so tell me why some economists were predicting a Japanese rebound late in 2013 when Mr. Abe took control of the country's central bank? Not even Mr. Abe can produce millions of new Japanese babies overnight! Still, everyone seemed to be thrilled that the prime minister was going to take power and try out some new experiments. They called his economic policy planning "Abenomics." I was far from impressed.

His idea was to bring inflation back to the normal level of 2%. I can understand that, and the man's willingness to end the prolonged period of deflation and weakness his country has suffered for 20 years. However, when you took a closer look at his approach, it was easy to predict the long-term failure of his plan. The plan was to print new money (quantitative easing), and put new fiscal spending measures and growth initiatives in place. By doing so, the yen would be devalued and exports could start rising again. With the country so dependent on exports, that would help the domestic economy grow again, combined with new spending and growth measures. When central banks print money, their governments have to purchase that new money and offer bonds in exchange (a debt promise to repay one day) to the central bank. To keep it simple, the government has to add debt on top of the debt it already carries. In 2014, Japan had a debt-to-GDP level of 240%, meaning they owed 2.4x more than the total products and services the country produces every year. Japan's public debt has ballooned to more than 1 quadrillion yen (the numeral 1 followed by 15 zero). The nation's net liabilities have reached 142 percent of GDP in 2014. The government's bright idea to try to curb the large national deficit was to increase and ultimately double the sales tax from 5% to 8% in 2014, and to 10% in October 2015. I may be wrong, but it seems to me that when sales taxes skyrocket like that, people get depressed and don't feel like consuming. If I lived in Japan, I would be trying to reduce my expenditures, not increase them. What would you do? Something tells me their fiscal mess is so deep, they simply have no choice but to hike the sales tax.

Moreover, the devaluation of the yen was hardly the brilliant idea of the century, because Japan is an island where almost everything must be imported. The devaluation had a disastrous effect, driving up prices for absolute necessities like food by an average of 50% and energy costs by 70%. Major Japanese companies are still assembling their products in Japan, but fewer and fewer are manufacturing them there. A weaker yen is driving up the prices of all imported parts. Higher prices mean lower margins for big corporations. Lower margins for corporations means compressing costs and reducing staff. The big economic wheel is turning in the wrong direction. The government of Japan released an interesting and ultimately devastating statistic in September 2013. It basically revealed that 31% of Japan's citizens had no savings left. The year before the number had been 26%, and so it rose 5% in just one year. That is a scary stat, and reveals how quickly a situation evolves. Based on those numbers, we can conservatively gauge that in 2015 the percentage of Japanese with no savings left will sit around 40%. Wow! I will end this chapter by sharing the Japanese corporate capex. The capex or capital expenditure is the percentage of investment corporations make per semester. In the last semester of 2014, the Japanese capex was negative, sitting at -5.1%. This reveals the level of confidence business owners and managers have in the future prospect of their country. The consumption level was no better, at -5.1%. My prediction remains exactly the same as in my first book. I advise you to stay far away from Japan. The bad news, of course, is that we are all connected. Remember when the tiny nation of Greece got in trouble? I don't like to think negatively, but when I see what is going on in Japan there is no way to be positive. I hope sharing these darker observations has not dampened your mood.

The good news is that Japan is somewhat isolated financially. Almost all of their massive debt is held by the Japanese themselves. In theory, you can hold a debt you owe to yourself for eternity, at any level you wish. However, I would ask: can a debt-to-GDP ratio go from 240% to a 2000% level without it having consequences, even though you owe all the debt to yourself and don't depend on other creditors? Good question. I think that the yen at that level would have the value of a Third World currency. Of course, I am not an expert on what may happen, and things like that are almost impossible to predict. I am not certain that a crisis or default would create a devastating world domino effect. Still, the best solution for Japan would probably be to erase everything and start over. Unfortunately, the Japanese have historically been reluctant to lose face that way. It would mean the country would have to take a financial step backwards, but instead, Japan is like a bankrupt man who still lives and acts like a millionaire as long as he can, even though he is broke. The perfect song for this chapter is: Big in Japan, by Alphaville.

VISION OF THE FUTURE

Every billionaire eventually comes up with a vision of the future before everybody else does. He then acts on that vision and implements it as quickly as possible to make the most of the market and become the leader in a chosen category.

When I was 10, *Back to the Future* was my favorite movie. It was amazing and fascinating to imagine the future from that perspective. Do you remember Doc Brown setting the dates in the car from 1985 to 2015 in Part Two of the trilogy? Well, we have now arrived in 2015, so we can judge if the moviemakers' vision synchs up with today's world. You have to admit, not much of what they imagined has really happened in the ensuing 30 years. The floating skateboard (the Hoverboard) impressed me, but as far as I know, it still doesn't exist. Cars still can't fly, and highways in the sky don't exist either. In my opinion, weather forecasts are no more accurate than they were in 1985 (in the movie, the weather forecast was accurate to the second). Clothes do not dry instantly, shoes don't lace themselves, and the food hydration oven is still only fiction.

On the other hand, they missed a lot of what *has* happened in our current world by missing the creation of the Internet, cellphones, iPads, etc... Also, most of our newspapers today are no longer read in a paper format (which was still the case in the movie). *Back to the Future* remains my favorite movie trilogy ever, because the future is fascinating and hard to master. Trying to predict the future is hugely difficult, mainly because we see the future through the lens of the present. Since this book is about becoming a billionaire, and billionaires are visionaries, let's conduct this exercise now and check back in five years to see if we were right. We will revisit the book or conduct a follow-up in books or articles to be published in the future.

So let's play a little prediction game here, even though we know we will probably be wrong most of the time. It's relatively easy to say universities will be fully mobile and online. Large, costly real estate campus buildings will probably be obsolete or transformed into condos! The guy or gal who develops the next great Internet university course will probably win big. Car will all run on hydrogen or something better. We already have great electric cars available, but better ones will be on the way. We will finally be on the right track to ridding ourselves of petroleum.

We will spend our vacations in outer space instead of going to Mexico! Honestly, though, I think I will always prefer spending time on a real beach. SpaceShipOne is already running, and we can be certain the experience will only get better, safer and cheaper. Long-distance galactic travel could become possible. Paper will be considered obsolete… except for use in the toilet. This could be the best possible news for our forests. The trees will probably be grateful for the end of clear-cutting, and in return might even provide us with a lot more clean oxygen. Most pharmaceutical drugs could become obsolete, since someone may invent a new machine that can diagnose and treat us. 3D printing machines are already widely available and cheap. You can download any program and build an incredible amount of useful objects and devices at will. As you can see, the future is full of opportunities. All we have to do is choose whether or not we want them in our lives. Those who introduce these new mass-market products will be rewarded in a big way. And you don't need to already be rich to participate in this evolution and make money as well. All you need is the flair to find these corporations on the stock market, which is the subject of our next chapter. The stock market is a fascinating arena where you don't need a lot of money to buy a few shares of a company you think will re-invent the wheel in its category and become the next Microsoft. The perfect song for this chapter is: Open the Door (To Your Heart), by the popular Van Morrison.

THE STOCK MARKET

Do you invest in the stock market? Please read that word carefully: invest, not speculate. There is an enormous difference between the two. Personally, I like to invest, and I hope you feel the same way.

The stock market is one of the most fantastic places on Earth. If you study its history, one of the more prominent names you will discover is Europe's Rothschild family. The most popular, highest-profile member of the family was Nathan, who lived in England. He liked to spend all day hanging around the floor of the London stock exchange. He was easy to find. Rothschild was a very patient man and perfectly understood how fear and greed worked in human nature. His favorite move was to invest against the current of the masses. He was also very good at starting false rumors to spark new financial panics. That way, he could buy tons of cheap bonds and stocks, then re-sell them for massive profits when market confidence returned. At one point in time, this family controlled half of the wealth on Earth. Some people claim the same may be true of the current Rothschild generation. I highly doubt it, but if so, they do a very good job of hiding all that money. If you asked me, I would tell you that I have made good money on the stock market. However, I've also stayed away from it for long periods of time. I was involved in the '90s, when it was easy to make money without knowing much about the market. I then realized that I could make more money by starting my own business. Later, in 2009, I once again saw that money could be made given the depressed state of the U.S. real estate market. The stock market was a bonanza at that time, with U.S. big bank stocks selling for peanuts. I bought Bank of America stocks and many others, but my real focus at that time was real estate. I simply realized that I could make a 30% return on my money every year, and absolutely nothing can beat that. In my first book, I said I had no plans to return to the stock market before 2020, but I will likely change my mind and return in 2015. You may wonder why I would do so when stocks are at their record-breaking highest.

My response is that I think we have reached the point when everything is about to change, that a couple of businesses are well-positioned to win a big chunk of the market, and of course the money that comes with it. I like the stock market so much because it is relatively passive. Nobody calls me to complain about operational problems at my stock manufacturing plant. Owning stocks is exactly the same as having your own business – without the operational issues. On the other hand, you have very, very little control over the key day-to-day decisions and course direction affecting the stocks you own. I never wait for the timing to be right before investing in the stock market; I prefer to focus on the prospects of each company. For instance, it may be advisable to pay a high price for a company stock if it will multiply its business and profits by a factor of 15 in the years to come. If so, that would be the easiest and best move of your life – an absolute home run. I am not a day trader, just as I am not a real estate flipper (except when it comes to producing a TV show like Flipping in the USA). I believe most value is created and unleashed over time. You simply have to write down your plan and goals, just as you did in your business plan. If you buy stock in a corporation involved in the paper industry, you must have a strategy behind your move. Is it because you still like the print version of a newspaper and believe it can succeed in the future? As you can see, you must have a sound betting strategy. When I bought Bank of America stock for pennies on the dollar in 2010, my strategic belief was that the government could not let it collapse no matter how bad the economy was. I also knew banks tend to know how to make money and recover fast, especially the biggest bank in America. I wrote down my scenario with a 2-year timeframe. sticking to the plan was easy. I had my investment scenario, my reasons and my timeframe, and the bet turned out to be successful. I had sound reasons for investing, and time proved me right. I sold my stock two years later for a nice profit. I might, of course, think that I sold the stock too quickly and could have made more money… but on the other hand, I stuck to my original plan and won anyway. To me, that is the most important element.

If you invest your money in stocks and have no idea of what I call the Where/Why/Timeframe plan, my guess is you're just looking to make a quick, easy buck. If so, your stock market trip will end up in a town called Nowhere, or worse: in Broke City. If you want to lose money with class, go to Las Vegas – at least you'll have a great time doing so. Otherwise, you need to be serious when the time comes to consider entering the stock market. There are plenty of books offering information on the process and the mechanics. At the end of the day, however, I think it all comes down to having a clear idea of what the future will hold, and acting on your vision by investing in companies that operate in the right domains and make good financial sense. Time will do the rest. Don't worry, stick to your plan, and do yourself a favor: don't change your mind with every passing day. You don't even need to check the daily stock price. Remember, time will tell you if your original plan was the right one.

If you remember just one thing, make it this: the stock market is the only place where you can buy a company without the need to buy land, factories, staff, offices, etc... If you don't have enough money to start your own company, you at least have the option to buy a fraction of a stock market corporation that is already operational and making sales. Remember, even if you only buy one share of Nike, you own a fraction of a leading corporation. You can claim it as yours, because that's true. You may be one of the smallest owners or stockholders of this goliath, but you are an owner nonetheless. Oh, and then there's the transaction fee. We live in a very interesting century, when transaction fees seem to have virtually disappeared. I remember buying my first stocks at the age of 16. The transaction fee then was $50 to buy, and the same to sell – and that was back in 1991. The whole process cost a minimum of $100. Adjusted to inflation, that would be equal to at least $175 today. I think we live in an interesting time, because today that transaction would cost less than $20. Follow the downward curve, and it will probably cost $1 or even nothing five years from now. Think about it, a $10 fee to own a fraction of a leading corporation. That's cheap, as is the $10 to finally sell it off when you get tired of it. What kind of company do you want to own? That's the kind of question you must ask yourself. Do you have a strategy in mind? Can you do this on your own, or do you need outside help? Believe me, if you can't do it on your own, tons of self-described experts will be happy to do it for you. I will further inform you that their "expertise" consists mainly in charging you fees, along with other industry techniques. You can do better without them, if you trust and believe in yourself.

When it comes to my money, the only expert who touches it is me. I call this my absolute Hands Off or I Break Your Arm approach. There is no expertise I can't compensate for or match myself – none at all. You should think the exact same way. Don't let others tell you what you should do. Period. Begin with the idea that you can learn how to do anything. Last year, I started to paint at home for the first time. Everybody laughed when I told them. They're not laughing anymore. This past summer, my wife and I rented a Winnebago for a 7-day holiday. My brother-in-law laughed, saying I would hit everything in my path. I drove that monster like I'd been doing it my whole life, and hurt absolutely nothing. Strangely, nobody laughs about it anymore. Some people pay a technician to deal with the seasonal opening and closing of their outdoor underground pool; believe me, if I had to learn how to do it myself, I would, and I would get it done. I think you must act in the exact same manner. Remember that deep down inside, I am still that little kid at school, very average, small of stature, going unnoticed, with no particular advantages at all... The only thing that set me apart was noticing along the way that we can do anything we may at first think is impossible.

Learning and mastering the stock market is also a one-way ticket to wealth. However, you need discipline, a vision of the future, sound reasons for choosing every single corporation you invest in, and moreover, you need a precise investment timeframe. Time is your best friend when it comes to turning your original vision into value. It's not very complicated, but also not that simple. I guess it's just like everything else in life. Naturally, when you consider investing your hard-earned money in your own business or the stock market, you need to have a bit of a 'gambler' inside of you…but consider the potential rewards of the process. The natural learning curve will also help you when your vision is off. I have a lot of great stories to tell about my experiences in the stock market. Here is the story of my worst experience. Ten years ago, I lost almost all my capital in a company involved in researching a new cancer product. And the only person I had to blame was: myself. It was a small $3000 investment, but I forgot to do my homework, to set goals for why I was investing in the company, or set a timeframe. I just went with a gut feeling and gambled – and "gambling" is what happened, with a losing result.

I like to learn things as I go through this life, and I am not blind to my mistakes. That bad investment cost me 90% of my capital. The best way to succeed is by learning, and I am no different. By the same token, I did not abandon the stock market because of that tiny loss. I know perfectly well that there are amazing investments right here and now, just waiting to be discovered. Many people have become wealthy through the stock market because they knew what they were doing. We can generate results that are just as good if not better if we really want to. We are the new Rothschilds of our time. I hope I have succeeded in communicating my passion and sparking your interest in seriously exploring this arena, where everything is possible.

Owning a successful business on the stock market is closer than you think.

CENTRAL BANKERS OF THE WORLD

The central bankers are supposed to be our friends. They hold in their hands the incredible power to print new money – as much as necessary. I must say, I wouldn't mind having that power; how about you? In all sincerity, I think we would do a better job – in terms of transparency, at the very least. Remember, central bankers also have the power to withdraw liquid money from the system in the event that inflation goes rocketing up.

Have you noticed that central bankers never have much to say when called upon to address and justify their actions? They never go into detail, they use complex terminology, and in the end, the journalists covering their media events don't even understand the meaning of the message. Why do they use terms that regular citizen can't understand? Why use words like "quantitative easing" instead of "printing new money from out of nowhere"? Do they have something to hide? You can find a lot of conspiracy theories on the subject online, and I must admit, they can seem plausible and nonsensical at the same time. I would ask every American this question: why are the names of the owners of the U.S. Federal Reserve the best-kept secret on Earth? The Federal Reserve is a private institution, the same way my Tim Hortons franchises are my property. Who the hell owns the Federal Reserve, and why would they keep that information hidden at all costs? If the theory on the Rothschilds is right and they still own half of the world's wealth, I would guess they hide behind the Federal Reserve by owning it (with a few of their best friends). After all, it is the absolute best business to own on Earth. They control the issuing of money. When they buy U.S. treasuries (at will), taxpayers (meaning all Americans) have to pay interest on them. To come out looking like the good guys, they return a great percentage of that collected interest to the U.S. treasury, but they also keep an undisclosed amount for themselves. Washington has nothing to say about this and cannot rule over or regulate them. They conduct their business beyond the reach of the system and its regulators. Let's be honest: only a massive revolution like the Boston Tea Party could possibly change the situation. The Federal Reserve is simply too powerful. And when the going gets rough, they have an easy way out: they just send us more money (and collect more interest by doing so). Basically, central bankers exist to stabilize the financial system when things get complicated. We witnessed this in action in the midst of the U.S. financial crisis in 2008. The Federal Reserve was instrumental in stabilizing public fears of a total meltdown and breakdown of the financial system. It is in their interest to keep the system running as smoothly as possible. Of course, we would all have a lot to lose in the event of a system breakdown.

What would happen in the event of an uncontrollable worldwide collapse? Nobody knows, because nothing like that has ever happened on a global scale. However, we can logically conclude that those with gold and silver holdings would win big. Gold and silver were used as money for thousands of years. If there were no other options, that could be the temporary substitute for a while. Do you keep physical gold and silver coins under your mattress? I think it's a good idea to keep a small amount at hand, just in case. Next Christmas, perhaps you can ask for silver coins instead of gifts with no intrinsic value. Holding too much of it is probably unnecessary, because people are pretty capable of finding new solutions to problems as they arise. Gold and silver would only be useful for an interim period while the right new solution was developed and implemented. Given the existence of the Internet, we could possibly create a new virtual worldwide legal currency overnight if we so desired. Let's return to the central bankers. Over the past 5 years, they've been very busy buying back bonds from the chartered banks. It wasn't a bad idea; in fact, it was quite logical. The idea behind this was to buy bonds from the regular banks and in return, provide them with liquidity – lots of liquidity. The central bankers thought that if banks had liquidity, they would grant new loans to business entrepreneurs and newlyweds looking to buy a new home.

New loans would mean new money in the system and the real economy. New money would mean new jobs and more activity, with a happy citizenry working, eating, drinking and spending. As in the time of the Roman Empire, the simple recipe to keep the system running was: give them bread and circuses. The same recipe still works well today. Over the past five years, the central bankers have expanded the money base to spark the economy into renewed activity.

The problem is that businessmen and women (don't forget women) are generally not in the mood to contract new loans when sales prospects are depressed. When you are active in the business world, you always try to look several years ahead to evaluate what your needs will be. In boom years, we invest, because we think our sales can only go in one direction: up. In tough times, we tend to think things will only get worse, and therefore cut back on expenses. In those periods, people aren't considering taking out new loans. Instead, they try to pay them down faster. Even if the banks have tons of cheap money, they can't force people to take out new loans. The same is true for the newlywed couples. If they think the economy is shaky, they will not buy that new house. As a result, the central bankers' strategy has not worked, because consumer confidence is not strong enough. If we don't act by taking out new loans, the regular banks end up sitting on huge piles of liquidity and the real economy does not benefit. In other words, the central bank activity of the past five years has not worked out the way they told us it would. Going to the other extreme, when the economy is booming and expanding on its own and consumer confidence is soaring through the roof, you must nonetheless still be careful. Inflation will generally rise during the boom times. To control the inflation, the central bank will raise interest rates and withdraw money from the system by selling back bonds to the chartered banks in exchange for their liquidity. That is how the central bankers control and limit liquidity in the system. It's important to be aware of how the system works. If you take out too many leveraged loans during good times, you can end up in the danger zone when interest rates rise and money in the system simultaneously becomes scarce. The economy can go from prosperous to middling very quickly, and you don't want to be in a position where you can end up in a tight squeeze.

This is another chapter offering you the opportunity to make wise decisions that will help you hold on to your wealth in any economic period or cycle. I know a businessman in Arizona who became incredibly wealthy during the real estate boom before 2008, accumulating a net worth of 200 million dollars, only to lose everything afterwards. I'd rather never have known what it means to be rich than to fly that high, only to crash back down to zero. Becoming wealthy is one thing; staying rich no matter how the economy turns is quite another. Those who remain wealthy for the long haul perfectly understand how the system works. They also know the central bankers can be their best and worst friends at the very same time. Sometimes, the central bank will choose the lesser of two evils because it causes less overall pain for the masses. I certainly don't want to suggest that central banks are evil.

I know they sometimes have very little choice in the decisions they make. Do you feel that you know more than you did before reading this chapter? I'm aware that not everybody loves reading about financial systems; still, people should, simply because we are all affected by the decisions made within them. Interest rates are critical. We are very fortunate right now, because with rates near zero, we know they can only go up. We are lucky to be living in a period of time when interest rate have been so low for so long, but many people have abused the situation by over-leveraging, believing that the ride will last forever. Trust me, it will not. I always prepare for the next wave of opportunity, and you should too. When interest rate rise again, many, many, many individuals and businesses will be in trouble, risking default. Opportunity will come knocking again. If you have cash and liquidity set aside instead of endless leverage, debt and loans, you will win. Now that you know, you have no reason not to prepare properly. Our chapters on financial systems are coming to a close. Can we live without central bankers? I don't think we can, because when a crisis in confidence occurs, they are there to calm everyone's nerves and relieve stress.

However, I do believe every central bank should be owned exclusively by the government of its country (and therefore, by its citizens). This model exists in Canada, and many other countries. A small group of individuals should never have the power to own a central bank in a country like the United States. To me, that's way too much power concentrated in the hands of a few (less than 10 people). Trust me, they are the true masters of the world. Compared to them, the President of the United States is practically powerless.

WHICH VERSION OF YOU?

Don't worry – we are still flying high in the sky. In fact, we have gained altitude and are higher than ever before. It would be magical to stay here forever and never come down, wouldn't it? I know that would be somewhat dangerous, but I like the idea.

This chapter is about you. I would like to know which version of your life you are in right now. Does that seem like a strange question? I think we pass through different versions of ourselves, depending on where we are and where we want to go. Do you feel the life you lived 20 years ago has almost nothing to do with your current one? Do you think it might be possible to move through different versions of ourselves?

Version 0.0 as a kid

Version 0.5 when you first entered school

Version 0.7 when you got your first job

Version 1.0 when you first kissed your loved one

Version 1.1 when you got your first professional job

Version 1.2 when you married your loved one

Version 1.3 when you bought your first house

Version 1.4 when you took your first vacation in Mexico

The list goes on and on, and I hope you have reached version 2.0 of yourself. Did you stop at one specific version number somewhere along the road and spend years there? If you study life and human nature, you already know we are only happy when we are growing. It doesn't matter if you are taking a new Zumba dance class or starting a new business, the drive is the same: the need to feel we are growing and moving forward.

Try to establish which version you are in right now – and more importantly, how long you have been there. Don't you want to move on to the next one? Of course you do; after all, we are all the same. Can we move on to the next higher version together? Teamwork seems to be more effective, as I learned at Tims. I know it's scary at first, because we don't know what that version will look like. Remember, we are in the same boat. What if that version ends up being incredibly rewarding? What if we could double or triple our income and make the people around us happier at the same time?

As in a game of Snakes and Ladders, we can always slip back down to an older version, for any number of good or bad reasons, but let's be honest – it's no fun. When I play Snakes and Ladders, as in real life, I am only happy when I am climbing. Then again, I never quit if I happen to slide back down. Quitters never win; I just turn my focus and energy back to climbing higher again. That's the way I play Snakes and Ladders, and the way I play in life. If you'd like, I will share the current version of my life. I have now reached the 2.0 version of me. My first book described the versions between 0.0 and 1.9. I started the book when I was 5 years old, when people constantly asked me: what would you like to do in your future life? I ended the book with Version 1.9 by explaining how I was building my real estate portfolio. I remained at version 1.9 for a couple of years. I felt I was not ready to go beyond that point at the time. My comfort zone had been firmly established. It's relatively easy to stay in your comfort zone and tell yourself you have succeeded enough and don't need to do anything more. That pattern can work for a period of time, but the question – what's next? – will always pop up one day or another. Without my realizing it at first, Diamond Heads changed everything. For the first time, I was starting a new business from scratch. This was new to me, and was the beginning of my own version 2.0 – a version virtually unlimited in its potential. Diamond Heads has the potential to grow into a global success, with many different product lines. Writing this book was also a new step. We can call it Version 2.1. It was a fun project, and I accomplished it quickly. My question for you remains the same. Which version of your life are you at now? How long have you been there? Can we help you achieve more? Can we help you get to the next version level? You're the only one who can answer these questions. You know yourself and your personal needs better than anyone else. If you are happy where you are right now, that's fine too. We all have different ideas about the level of achievement we want to reach in life.

However, if you've been frustrated for years by your current version, then that's a different story. Do you know exactly why you are stuck in this version? Do you know what's stopping or blocking you from moving to the next one?

How long will you to stay in this current version until you finally decide: enough is enough? If you ask yourself the right questions, you will receive the right answers. Then, you must decide what to do with them. A total turnaround may be appropriate if you are looking for different results. I know that's hard to accomplish, but it is also what I am currently doing. In a way, you are not alone in this journey to the New Version of Me. The perfect song for this chapter is: You and I, by John Legend. You and I are looking and searching for the higher versions of ourselves.

FOLLOW-UP ON THE LAW OF ATTRACTION

This book is a by-product of the Law of Attraction. Yes, you read that right. Having said that, I don't consider myself to be a specialist on the subject. I am more what we would call an adept and happy daily user.

Strangely, on the very same day I decided it was time to get serious about starting to write, I spoke to an author who has written more than 20 books. Her name is Slavica Bogdanov. She is a specialist in the Law of Attraction and other subjects. If you want to read an entire volume or two on the subject, I suggest you pick up one of her great books. Her latest is *From Bankrupt to Wealthy*. Because the Law of Attraction likes speed, I started to write the first page of my book the very same day of that conversation. I took the encounter as a perfect sign from the universe. If you believe strongly in the universe and the Law of Attraction, you already know you have to interpret any sign as a message to Go, Go, Go. The universe will never speak to you directly, with words. Answers are sent via coincidences and signs. If you observe them properly, the universe will provide you with all the answers you're waiting for.

Having a gut feeling is your best friend, and you must use it daily. We all have gut feelings, but we rarely act in harmony with them. When your gut feeling vibrates in harmony with your choices, you will feel that accomplishing them is very easy and natural. Since I began writing this book, my gut feeling has told me one single thing: keep writing, you're doing great so far. When I was not writing, my gut feeling became lonely, and sent a different message: when are we going to write again? It's been just that easy for the past 3 weeks now. Believe me, never in my wildest dreams would I have ever thought I could write so quickly. My second book project had been on ice for a year and a half; then, out of nowhere, boom! There it was, well on its way! The only difficult thing I'd had to do was take the first step into action.

I urge you to act on the very same day you receive a sign from the universe. If you wait for the perfect time, you risk waiting forever. Next, you must write down the goals for your new project. Remember, only 2% of people do this. When we do things nobody else does, we become successful. I use these tools myself, so why wouldn't you? And that is exactly what I did. I carry a small sheet with me every day, upon which I had written: The Billionaire Right Next Door, my first worldwide bestselling book. I had also entered the amount of time required to finish the project. My first book took far too long to write and my family suffered a bit during the experience, so I decided I would finish this one in only a month. I was willing to consider a longer time span if I couldn't find a subject worth sharing. The universe sends me tons of ideas, one after another. I feel privileged and fortunate. Diamond Heads was also a product of the Law of Attraction. Remember, I had been searching like crazy for the perfect name for the new brand and suddenly, when I was almost ready to give up, the answer popped up in front of me.

Can we really attract what we desire? What do you think? Do you have a great story about the Law? If the answer is yes, I would like to hear it. I love hearing success stories about the Law. Plenty has been said and written on the subject, but what is the true answer? I am a big believer in it, because I have 20 different personal stories that have worked out perfectly well in harmony and accordance with this Law. Believing in the Law of Attraction is almost the same as having faith. You have to decide whether you have faith or not. Those who believe are right; and those who do not believe are also right. Again, it's up to you to choose which side you are going to be on. Remember that, either way, you will be right... but I prefer the first camp, where everything is possible. Those who don't believe they can do anything to attract what they want in life are often attracting something else: misery, and everything they don't necessarily want. It's easy to blame your spouse, your child, your boss, God, etc. for your misfortune... but what if you were, in fact, the only person to blame?

The day you understand that you are the only person responsible for your life is the day you save yourself a lot of time and frustration. When that happens, we can start looking for solutions instead of laying blame. That's why I like to be surrounded by people who have a positive and ambitious mind. That kind of energy is contagious and helps me focus and stay on the right track. Always remember that we can easily be contaminated by negative thinking and destructive thoughts. The perfect song for this chapter is: It's All Coming Back to Me Now, by Celine Dion. Please embrace the Law of Attraction; it's your one-way ticket to the life you dream about. You will, of course, have to master and re-master this simple but easily forgotten Law each and every day. It's hard to admit this truth to ourselves, but we are the 100% sole creators of our lives. Let's build them into what we really want them to be.

SETTING UP YOUR PLAN

Do you like to plan out your life? I pose the question because most of the people I know don't plan at all. They buy books on the subject, but don't follow through. To me, that's like buying a cookbook but never making a recipe.

If you were an engineer, I'm sure you would draw up serious plans before building a bridge. Why should it be any different when it comes to building success and wealth? The most successful day we ever had at my Tim Hortons store was the one we meticulously planned out at 4 a.m. before the morning rush. One day, you will be a guest in my home and I will show you how I plan – firstly, because I am proud of the way I do it, and secondly, because I want to show you what lies behind success. I like the Formula One analogy: When you look at the temporary guest seating at a race, all you see when facing the stands are the places where folks will sit and drink beer. Take a look behind the seats and you will see a huge amount of metal tubing built up into the infrastructure that keeps the seats securely upright and safely in place.

Believe me, success works in exactly the same way. Take a look behind anyone's success story and you will find a lot of infrastructure that keeps that success intact and moving forward. You will never find any success story without sound infrastructure in place. Every long-lasting success story has been planned out well. My question remains: do you seriously want to bring success into your life? If so, I would immediately ask to see your plan. You don't want to end up looking ridiculous, right? I would expect you to have already done your homework. If I ask you where you'll be in five years, you should have a ready answer and confidently share all the details on how you will get there. Otherwise, we are both wasting our time.

At the risk of being rude, let's say you went to the doctor, but couldn't tell him where it hurts. Do you think he'd be amused? Now, let's change places, with you asking me: Dany, where will you be five years from now? Right off the bat, I will tell you that I will be in perfect health, with my family enjoying life just as we do today. On the business side, I have already revealed my follow-up goals in my books. We learn by repetition. I will still be under contract with my Tims stores. My young son Vincent dreams of owning them one day, but we'll have to wait and see whether or not he ends up changing his mind as he grows up. Next, Diamond Heads will be racking up sales worldwide in 50 countries. We will be listed on the New York Stock Exchange, but will still own 51 percent of the shares. All the Diamond Heads master franchises for designated territories will be sold out in every country except, of course, for Hawaii.

I will officially be a billionaire. I will live in Hawaii full-time and play 50 rounds of golf a year on lovely ocean-side golf courses. I will conduct One-on-One Mastermind sessions at Diamond Head, attended by people from all over the world, but only when I have space in my agenda. I will exclusively drive electric cars, or those manufactured using even better technology. The annual Diamond Heads Mastermind events will be recognized as the absolute best in their field. The High Achievers Society will have one thousand exclusive, carefully selected members. At that point, we will consider launching a cruise with only High Achievers Society members on board. I hope you will be among them. What about the world literary competition? I think we can safely assume it will be a popular event – after all, a writer can win $100,000 just anywhere. No other contest even comes close to offering that prize amount. I predict that at least five thousand people will participate every year. Tremblay Realty in Florida will employ 50 real estate agents and sell 200 or more properties every year. Our office will be located in Palm Beach near the Flagler museum. Tremblay World will manage to find spots in my agenda so I can present lectures in places like Switzerland. I like skiing, and chocolate. Furthermore, I love the country in general, and its architecture. The Billionaire Right Next Door 5 will be my newest book. Indeed, it's probably a great idea to publish an entire series of Billionaire Right Next Door books. I'm guessing my publisher will love the idea.

I would like to offer you all the details on how I will reach these goals. Every aspect has being meticulously planned; however, sharing all that info would take up too much space and is beyond the scope of my mission in this book. Simply bear in mind that you have to use the same kind of planning and vision in your project. Even if you only have one goal, you should do things exactly the way I do. I don't expect you to have the same amount of goals. Fourteen years ago, my only goal was to become a businessman. My list was fairly small, but it was nonetheless the challenge of my life. I like to hand-draft my goals on big cardboard signs. Some people who've visited my home and seen them have told me that I may be good at drawing, but there's no way I will achieve my goals. Those people have no idea what I am capable of – and frankly, I don't care what they think. Other guests say I am visionary and ambitious. I tend to prefer that second group... I never hide my goals when guests come over to visit. I am not shy; my goals represent who I am and where I want to go. They are in perfect harmony with me. These planning tools will work for you, but you must be very serious in the way you use them. My Diamond Heads business plan has 10 pages of details spelling out how I will proceed to build the brand and succeed. You must do the same for all your projects and goals.

Try to fill in 10 pages of details, as I do. The more details, the better. You want your plan to be complete, without any bind spots. Don't worry about the money required for each goal – that's not your job for now. Remember, I was $75,000 short on the cash I needed for the down payment when I was planning to buy my first Tim Hortons location. Use your 10 pages to write down the different growth phases of your project. How many hours will you devote to this every week? How will you feel inside? What will be the impact on your family? What kind of products are you selling and what is your target market? How big is your market? What share of the market will you control? Is your business local or international? Are you selling online? How many staff members will you need in the different phases of growth? What are your repair costs? What profit margin will your products deliver? Who and where is your competition? What are the differences between you and them? Are you regulated by any government laws? If so, do you know the substance of these laws? You'll need to make estimates on most of those points. It's impossible to be accurate with estimates, but at the very least, you will likely be fairly close to the real-life demands. Planning is the opposite of dreaming. When you plan things out and write down every detail, your dream is suddenly transformed into a doable project – and that is entirely different. The perfect song for this chapter is: I Believe in You and Me, by Whitney Houston.

I am a firm believer in making plans. That may be due to the fact that I studied mechanical engineering. In mechanics, nothing works without clear and precise measurements and 3D drawings. My most valuable advice to you is to stop dreaming and start planning.

FINAL DESTINATION

I can see our final destination from the window. Have you enjoyed the trip so far? As we make our approach, we are slowly descending and dropping altitude. Our pilots seem to be both happy and exhausted. I think they did a great job, always correcting our trajectory to make sure we reached the right destination.

Incidentally, this destination is yours. We are not in Hawaii, at least not for now. Where are we exactly? I ask because you're the only one with the precise answer. What is your life destination? Are you living in a big waterfront home? Is it in America, or in a foreign country? Are you driving a car or flying a helicopter? How many kids do you have in your special destination? Who is your loved one; can you perfectly describe that person? I am happy and excited to be your main guest, since I have been waiting for this moment. Don't worry and don't be afraid, we are in a special dimension I like to call the vision of your future, where everything has taken off as planned. We will not be there for long, the time is short, so let me ask you a couple of questions:

Did you work hard to finally get to exactly where you wanted to be? Where and when did you reach your turning point? Did you change your job or business? Why did it take you so long to finally decide? Are you happy in this place, or do you still want more? How did you choose this perfect place? Did you seek out the help of a professional coach? Do you have new projects in mind? Are you still planning to climb higher, or will you just relax and enjoy yourself? Do you spend all day doing what you like to do? Do you have a private chef at home? Do you maintain a healthy diet? What is the water temperature of the ocean where you live? Are you a billionaire? If not, are you well positioned to become one soon? How many customers do you serve annually?

I like to know what drives people in life – it's my passion. We've run out of time and must step out of the vision of your future right now, but you can always extend it further as needed, when you're driving or just before you drift off to sleep. You have to keep your vision alive. Like a newborn baby, your vision of the future is always vulnerable. In fact, it only takes one negative person saying you are unrealistic to destroy your vision for good. Keep in mind: not everyone wants you to succeed. Be wary, because your vision is your personal treasure; it's worth billions, and you must protect it in every way possible. Thieves are everywhere. When people hear a great idea, their first thought is: how can I take that and use it myself before anyone else does? Protect your ideas until they are ready to be marketed. The best way to protect them is to discuss them only after papers have been signed or a copyright is in place. We are arriving at your future home, and I am impressed. I'd like to briefly extend our time spent in your vision of the future. Hey, even my house isn't this huge! Your property has beauty in every detail. I also appreciated finding two glasses of champagne waiting for us on your balcony facing the ocean. Your life appears to be an amazing success – congratulations, I'm proud of you. I would love to take a ride in your helicopter; I hope you've already planned out an aerial tour of your vineyard. Do you think I've gone too far with your vision? After all, it is *yours*. You simply need to tell me and I will tailor it to your specifications, but the fact remains the same: all this can actually become reality in a couple of years. I know and believe that anything and everything is possible; I have no doubts about what can be accomplished. In my mind, if we have a vision, then we can transform it into reality.

Returning to your vision, I am delighted to finally meet the love of your life. I only have one question: are you with the same person today that you were with when you first began your life turnaround? I ask because not all life partners like the idea of their significant other making a 180-degree life shift. I understand this can be somewhat destabilizing. Remember that making a dramatic life turnaround often means breaking up with your current life partner. I am fortunate, because my wife Chantal follows me almost everywhere I choose to go. That's not always the case with every couple. There are risks and rewards involved in this vision game. You can never be precisely certain of the final results of a life turnaround – that is absolutely true. On the other hand, if you never try, you will never experience the great things that await you. You are meant to have an amazing life: let the magic of your life begin. I am proud to see you have chosen to build your first business from scratch. Just look at your beautiful oceanfront home. I know the risk/reward curve was stressful at first (just as it was for me), but in the final analysis, your life turnaround did pay off, right? I am also proud to see you submitted your second business plan directly to Tremblay World via the official web site www.billionairerightnextdoor.com. Your business plan was so impressive that we became business partners! I know that our list of worldwide contacts was helpful from the get-go. I know you worked like crazy afterwards, but still, this was a great win-win deal. Do you think our vision of the future is exaggerated? If you think it is, then you are correct. If you think this is doable, you are also correct. You decide which camp you want to be in. Needless to say, many business plans fail from the very start; and believe me, I rarely choose them. I'm not saying I'm always right; I make mistakes in business, like everybody else. Usually, though, I am fairly good at predicting whether a business will fail or succeed. I am not here to propagate false expectations. If the business plan isn't ready, or the market isn't ripe for success, I will simply state the facts and explain my point of view.

Returning once again to your vision, I ask why you have a huge pool in your backyard when the ocean is so close. You respond: because I like it that way! When the ocean gets a little colder in January, you move into enjoying your pool. I briefly forgot that your pool is, of course, equipped with the latest and best in pool heaters. Your vision of the future is over, at least for now. Wouldn't it be nice to get serious and make it happen? Most of the initial decisions must come from your side. Once that has happened, we can get to work on you. Nothing is too big... once we erase the negative beliefs we carry with us every day, which block our progress. Let your desires run free as you imagine yourself in the driver's seat heading to your vision of a future life. Those desires and sentiments will create the magnetism and power needed to draw these things into your life. It's your life and your story; seize this as a rare opportunity to make the picture truly daring and different. We live in a unique time when anything is possible. Grab your own piece of the pie. We are approaching the end of this book, and I realize that tomorrow, I will no longer be writing it. Believe me when I tell you that the experience of writing The Billionaire Right Next Door has been so intense that tomorrow, I will probably feel a significant sense of loss. Something will be missing in my life. The opportunity to speak directly with you has been an immense privilege. I promise you that I would never take that privilege for granted. Remember that in my mind, I am still the humble little boy in high school whom nobody noticed. Back then, I always loved being called upon to speak in front of the class. Every time I stood in front of the class to speak, I captured the attention of all of my classmates. They would hang on my every word, and that's a feeling I have never forgotten. When you are good at something, you know it deep down inside. People are afraid of public speaking because they dread making a mistake. When I speak in front of people, I am myself, because after all I am unique... just like you. I have my unique French-Canadian accent and unique sense of humor, and everyone still enjoys what I have to say.

I'm sure you will miss me, and I hope to see you again soon. Hawaii would be the perfect meeting point, but we could do it anywhere else in the world. Paris is great if you enjoy perfectly flaky croissants. I can travel to wherever you live if it fits my schedule. As I write these lines, James Morrison is singing I Won't Let You Go live. There's yet another little coincidence delivered by the universe. I particularly like these lyrics: "If your sky is falling / Just take my hand and hold it / You don't have to be alone / I won't let you go." It's the perfect song for this chapter.

I hope you have decided to climb to the next level of your life. From there, anything is possible. If you still need time to decide, I respect that, too. We are all in different spots along the road of success. If you feel like you are still growing, congratulations, keep up the good work. The goal is to make the most of ourselves every day. Kids make the most of themselves when they learn to walk and dance for the first time; why should we stop just because we're grownups 30 years later?

I didn't need anybody's help on my road to success. Today, I can justly claim that I was a 100% self-made man. I'm not trying to show off here: my problem was that I didn't know anyone who could help me in my specific approach to success. Even today, I still don't have a real coach to guide me in the choices I make. Right up into the present day, nobody has ever been able to synch up with the way I think and where I want to go. I have friends who are successful, but they are just not like me. Frankly, I don't feel that I will need anybody's help in the future either. I know exactly what I want, and I will go right out and grab my slice of the pie... or cheesecake!

You may be like me – you may not need anybody to help locate your path to success. You can learn on your own every time you hit a bump in the road. On the other hand, if you would like to be guided, you should know that the option is always available. I would like to personally thank you. You have invested your time in reading this book and learning about how I have operated on a daily basis for the past 14 years. You now know everything about me; you know all my secrets. I can't hide anymore. The next time we meet, in person, we won't need to waste any time talking about me. And so we will only discuss you, and your projects. My guess is you have a lot of million-dollar projects sleeping in the back of your mind. I will be there to provide a spark and bring them to life.

I would like to end the chapter by sending you all my positive energy. After all, we can now consider ourselves friends. I wish you the very best, from the bottom of my heart. I don't like to say goodbye. I prefer: see you later (alligator)... and mark my words, you will miss me.

Sincerely,

Dany

SPECIAL THANKS

Unsurprisingly, I have a long Thank You list. Success only happens with great teamwork, and this is the only place I can acknowledge the hard work of many talented and generous people. As the years unfurl, my Special Thanks list will probably only get longer. Have you ever watched the Academy Awards and noticed how many people an actor thanks?

Many thanks to a couple of friends who seriously told me they saw me as the next Donald Trump (without the hairstyle, of course). That was an incredible source of motivation. I will do my very best to make this challenging vision a reality. Thanks to the family members who were there for me over the years, listening to different business plan scenarios. Thanks to the friends and family members who were the first buyers of Diamond Heads prototype products. We were stunned to see products selling simply on the basis of our written descriptions of them.

Thanks to everyone for your incredible enthusiasm for Diamond Heads, back when it was nothing but a fragile concept. Thank you for bringing the same level of enthusiasm to the idea and writing project that became The Billionaire Right Next Door. Thanks to Guillaume Lussier for his consummate dedication to making the first Diamonds Heads product lines available. Last month, he told me he was working extra shifts at night to make sure everything was perfectly on track. I'm always happy to encounter that level of devotion. Thanks to all my readers for your support of my first book. I hope you liked this one just as intensely. I will do my best to write the next one in 2016. Things evolve very quickly these days, and I want to keep you up to date. I think one book per year is the perfect ratio.

Thanks to my web designers, whom I was lucky enough to secure before they got too busy. Great talents create great websites.

Thanks to all my team members and partners. Great businesses can never be built with mediocrity.

Thanks to the universe for bringing me all that I want and ask for every day. You don't always send me things as I expected them, but I will never complain – you give me so much, and I will be forever faithful. I hope you are proud of me. I always try to make things happen.

Thanks to my own publishing company Tremblay World and the devoted staff behind. Thanks in advance to all the readers who will eventually submit their book projects to the Diamond Heads annual world literary competition. I expect it to be hugely successful in the future, and I can't wait to read your books. I wrote every single word in this book with passion and honesty. If you felt that, then my mission would be accomplished. The perfect song for this Special Thanks section is: When I'm With You, by Faber Drive. I don't like saying goodbye.

In fact, I would like to stay with you forever...

ABOUT THE AUTHOR

Born in 1975, Dany Tremblay comes from a loving middle class family in Montreal. His mother was a first grade teacher and his father was a small construction entrepreneur. At the age of 5, he already dreamt of being rich one day. He fell in love with the restaurant business the very day he started his first job as a dishwasher in a French restaurant called Le Crocodile.

He later spent four years earning a college degree in mechanical engineering. Armed with his new diploma, he seized upon available opportunities, working in such large aeronautics corporations as Bombardier and Pratt & Whitney. He worked in his field of study for five years, but as time passed, he realized his future was elsewhere.

With every passing day, Dany felt an increasingly powerful need to become his own boss. In 2001, he finally quit his job and bought his first new restaurant with his life partner, Chantal. Four years later, they bought a second new restaurant. In 2009, he started Tremblay Holdings, a new company created to acquire and manage a real estate investment portfolio. The company's natural buying strategy was to invest in a depressed U.S. real estate market, where opportunities were plentiful. The Tremblay Holdings portfolio now has investments in 6 U.S. states.

In 2013, he wrote and published his first book, entitled The 50 Secrets of My Success. The book became a bestseller in its first year of release. He and his wife Chantal created more companies over the years, including Diamond Heads International, involved in luxury goods. The world headquarters is located in Honolulu, Hawaii. He has a vision and business plan to grow the brand worldwide. For more information, please visit the official web site: www.diamondheads.co

His latest book, The Billionaire Right Next Door, was written and released in early 2015.

Tremblay World is the most recent addition to his family of companies, managing book publishing, conferences, speaking engagements, special events and book-related products available on the web site: www.billionairerightnextdoor.com

Today, Dany lives mainly in West Palm Beach, but he spends an increasing amount of time in Hawaii. Montreal is his family's third residence.